Too Much and Not the Mood

Too Much and Not the Mood

Durga Chew-Bose

Farrar, Straus and Giroux   New York

Farrar, Straus and Giroux
18 West 18th Street, New York 10011

Library of Congress Cataloging-in-Publication Data
Names: Chew-Bose, Durga, author.
Title: Too much and not the mood : essays / Durga Chew-Bose.
Description: First edition. | New York : Farrar, Straus and Giroux, 2017.
Identifiers: LCCN 2016041344 | ISBN 9780374535957 (paperback) |
    ISBN 9780374714680 (e-book)
Subjects: BISAC: LITERARY COLLECTIONS / Essays. | POETRY /
    American / Asian American.
Classifications: LCC PS3603.H49 A6 2017 | DDC 814/.6—dc23
LC record available at https://lccn.loc.gov/2016041344

Designed by Abby Kagan

Our books may be purchased in bulk for promotional, educational, or
business use. Please contact your local bookseller or the Macmillan Corporate
and Premium Sales Department at 1-800-221-7945, extension 5442, or by
e-mail at MacmillanSpecialMarkets@macmillan.com.

www.fsgbooks.com • www.fsgoriginals.com
www.twitter.com/fsgbooks • www.facebook.com/fsgbooks

5   7   9   10   8   6

For Dulcie, Felix, Amiya, Chameli

To my family and Sarah, and to hurrying home

I just had this one image of Jack Nicholson holding a pink balloon.

—POLLY PLATT

Contents

Contents

Too Much and Not the Mood

1

Heart Museum

THERE'S an emoji on my phone that I've never used, of a shell-pink tower-block building with blue windows. Smaller than an apple seed, crumb-sized—if that—it stands six stories high. Six windows going up: three square, three rectangular. I counted them and double-checked because extra-small things bring out the extra-small person in me who sometimes even triple-checks things; who still chances certainty might exist in asking, "Promise me?"

This emoji is further detailed with a letter *H*—pink too, but more or less magenta—that hangs on its front and is matched in size by a pink heart floating above the building's extension; like a shiny Mylar balloon escaping into the sky. The building's roof is maroon, and an awning, also pink, shelters its two-door entranceway. Unlike the "house" emoji, for instance, this one has zero greenery: no shrubs, no tree. No landscaping. Just a stand-alone building that, until recently, I thought stood for "Cardiologist." The *H* and its accompanying heart were an expression of, in my mind, *heart hospital.* Or heart doctor. And not, as I later discovered while scrolling through an emoji glossary on-line: "Love Hotel." I was sure the building stood for all matters having to do with that four-chambered, fist-shaped muscle we carry—that carries us—with constancy. That beats—did you know?—more than one hundred thousand times a day.

Imagine that. Even when we're pressing snooze and rolling over in bed, folding ourselves into our covers and postponing the day's bubbling over, and soon after notching cold butter on warm toast, or later coming to a halt as we bound up a flight of subway stairs only to stall behind an elderly woman whose left leg trails behind her right leg—one leaden step at a time—even then, when time decelerates and the relative importance of *our* lives, of *our* hurry, undergoes a sudden, essential audit; even then, our heart never stops.

Even when a name I've long ignored—blotted from my mind in order to safeguard some good sense—pops up bold in my inbox. Even when I notice three consecutive missed calls from my father and, as if metronomed by doom, fear the worst, my heart does not stop beating.

Even when I *hear a sound* or count footsteps following me at night, or spot two rats darting from a pile of trash, or hold my breath as Lisa Fremont climbs the fire escape to Thorwald's apartment while Jeff anxiously sits guard in his wheelchair, watching with his binoculars from across the courtyard. *Even then*. Even Hitchcock. Despite pure movie fright—how it skewers me—my heart doesn't stop.

Even when the cab all of a sudden breaks and jerks forward. When anything lurches. Careens. When "Think fast!" trails the toss. When my leg involuntarily twitches and I sense I've lost my balance, only to wake up having dozed off. Even when I watched *Man on Wire*, bewildered as to why anyone would perform such a stunt. Eight passes back and forth. A quarter mile up.

Even when a thought springs fresh in my mind on the subway and solves an essay I'd just about abandoned. On the rare occasion my subconscious welds, language has a gift, I've learned, for humiliating those luminous random acts of creative flash into impossible-to-secure hobbling duds. The best ideas outrun me. That's why I write.

Even in June 2011, when my roommate and I paused Game 4 of the Heat–Mavericks Finals because: *CRASH!* The sound—the loudest, most intense crinkle—traveled from my bedroom at the front of our apartment, which faced the street. We'd only lived there, on the second floor, maybe two or three months. As we walked slowly down the length of our long hallway, I noticed my window was broken, the glass veined. A single hole in the bottom corner. Flattened on my floor near my bed were the pummeled shards of a bullet. Some kids on the street, my neighbors later told me, had been playing with a gun. My heart clamped and didn't recoup for days. I slept on the couch, not out of fear—I don't think—but because, no matter how diligently I swept, I kept finding slivers of glass on my floor. They seemed to suggest it's okay to be someone who is slow to move on.

Even when pointe shoes flit down the stage like muffled hazard. When a fur coat slides off a woman's bare shoulders. Or when a kiss on my neck obscures all clichés about kisses on necks and I am no longer human but merely an undulation.

Or when Mariah pleats a litany of notes into "Vision of Love." When her finale crests and becomes tendency. Even then, my heart upholds.

Or those first ten seconds of "Man in the Mirror." Right before Michael sings, *I'm gonna make a change*, and those early notes sound like crystal snowflakes falling on sheets of sugar. Or my favorite: the undervalued "Who Is It." Jealousy's anthem. How it thumps. How it's obsessed. Paranoid. How it's frantic enough to summon past jealousies, no matter how beyond them you think you are. "Who Is It" is a maze. It's the sound of being stuck in one. It's the pursuer feeling pursued. Betrayal can debilitate but it can also animate. It's how even at one's most suspicious, the heart speeds up—ticks, twitches, is a grenade—yet never stops.

Or when I meet someone new who loves a movie just as I've loved that movie; who speaks at such a clip about it— tenderly, contagiously—that I forget to speak at all and smile like a fool because, now and then, meeting new people isn't so terrible.

Even when the ATM reveals my bank balance unsolicited. When a stranger's ringtone is the same as my morning alarm, waylaying me with acute dread midafternoon. When life's practicalities knock the romance out, and money, time, sense syndicate my passions into bills, deferred goals, and all the boring bits.

Even when a buzzer-beating shot bounces on the rim. When Steph sinks a no-look. When Kerri Strug landed her pained, team-winning second vault at the 1996 Olympics and I watched with my eyes half covered, sitting on the floor of my aunt's Atlanta home, not far from the Georgia Dome.

Even when I'm startled by an object flying in my periphery. Dust. Refracted light. Anxiety's UFOs. Or when a *GASP!* is disproportionate to why I've gasped, my heart continues, as ever, pulsing toward its daily quota. More than one hundred thousand times a day. Eighty beats per minute.

Even when I stand naked in my room after a long day of stupid letdowns, when I consider becoming a woman who screams or hacks off her hair, or tosses her purse instead of hanging it. Even then, when nakedness can't undo the day, when my heart is lodged in my throat and my whole body falls limp—my whole body like my left wrist when I fasten my watch with my right hand. Limp like that. Even then, when I feel completely poured out and defeated. A Dyson in the desert.

Or what about the day MCA died. My heart seemed to chasm because the Beastie Boys were—I'm not sure how best to say this—one of many attributes, albeit a critical one, that firmly positioned me as a younger sister. They were the music my brother listened to with his door closed. The CD he wouldn't let me borrow. Still now, on those hot summer days when the sun lacquers Manhattan storefronts into something aureate and amber-rich, when the air is impenetrable, blistered, and rank, and when brick tenements on Ludlow evoke whatever decade speaks to your nostalgia, my brother's copy of *Paul's Boutique* comes to mind. What I perceived back then in its cover art was the possibility of New York, New York: a city so in possession of itself that I fathomed an entire kingdom in those five-by-five inches.

Even that winter long ago, when I was running late to a holiday dinner at my friend's apartment, clueless as to where I'd jotted down her new address but feeling somehow lovely because I was in a hurry, wearing tights that cinched my waist like a secret tension under my shift dress, and bell sleeves that gave me extra wingspan to *sail around the corner*. Mid-scramble, my then-boyfriend rattled off my friend's street name from memory, without even looking up from his book, as if he'd been to her place before. Even then, despite the wrench of good instinct—that queasy wave of it—of learning young that having a hunch is, like so many female facets, both misery and boon. Even when I said nothing because *Why start something?* he'd say. Is there anything less clear than an accusation made when you're running out the door? When those fault lines inside of us quake on account of all that is built up and unkempt between two people in love—on account of perceptiveness and wariness resembling in tone. Even then, when I felt tremendously sad in my lovely dress, my heart did not stop.

Even when I'm caught off guard by a lathery shade of peach on the bottom corner of a painting at the Met, as if being reminded that I haven't seen all the colors, and how there's more to see, and how one color's newness can invalidate all of my sureness. To experience infinity and sometimes too the teasing melancholy born from the smallest breakthroughs, like an unanticipated shade of peach, like Buster Keaton smiling, or my friend Doreen's laugh—how living and opposite of halfhearted it is. Or my beautiful mother growing out her gray, or a lightning bolt's fractal scarring on a human body, or Fantin-Latour's hollyhocks, or the sound of someone practicing an instrument—the most sonically earnest sound. Or how staring at ocean water so blue, it leaves me bereft. In postcards, I'll scribble "So blue!" because, what else?

Or even when I hear a recording of Frank O'Hara recite "Having a Coke with You," gleefully anticipating him saying *yoghurt,* saying *flu-o-rescent orange tulips.*

      I listen
      to him and I would rather listen to him than all
            the poets in the world
      except possibly for Dorothy Parker occasionally
            and anyway she'd hate that

Or the first time I saw Jackie cry. It was December. She was moving to San Francisco, so we spent the day strolling around midtown, stopping at the Rockefeller tree and pointing up at its peak, curious as to how it stood so big. Wondering how trees are made to look immovable once they've already been displaced. In Bryant Park we talked about manatees because I'd recently seen an ad in a magazine to adopt one. "For the Holidays," the ad proposed. "Nature's Precious Treasures." Jackie and I both agreed how naturally forlorn manatees look—like underwater shar-peis stuck in some forever torpor. Like they'd already surrendered themselves to their endangered fate. For half a block we pondered adopting one and sharing custody, because when friends move away, what else is there to talk about? Nothing material feels very good. I walked Jackie back to her studio in Woodstock Tower and watched her pack some boxes and determine whether she should leave behind a lamp. I considered taking a pair of purple three-pound weights she was getting rid of. Would I use them? Probably not. But they were purple. And talking about taking them was yet another way of not talking about Jackie leaving. I teased her for deciding to schlep a rusty step stool across the country. She insisted it held sentimental value. It was clear to us we were both in slow motion, appreciating the other person for little reasons, refusing to say goodbye, formally. When I finally did leave, in haste, I realized I'd forgotten my earphones on her bed, and when I hurried back from the elevator and knocked on her apartment door, Jackie answered in tears. Together, in that moment, we could have probably adopted a hundred manatees. Easy.

I've felt infinity too, late in my twenties, when I discovered a word in English I'd only ever known in Bengali. Or when I spot, with hours still left in the day, the moon's hazy thumbprint. How the moon enjoys debunking the day. Or when I clutch my Playbill as I exit the theater, regretful that I don't see more plays. I'm so vitalized in those seconds— all set to gulp more, to not speak but to stand under the marquee bulbs and grab the arm of my companion as if corroborating impact—that I'm certain, if I wanted, I could walk home from West Forty-seventh, across the bridge and back to Brooklyn. That spiked measure of awe—of *oof*—feels like a general slowing, even though what's really taking place is nothing short of a general quickening. The sheer, ensorcelled panic of feeling moved. Infirmed by what switches me on but also awake and unexpectedly cured. Similar to how sniffing a lemon when I'm carsick heals.

Or marveling at the bull's-eye patterns in a malachite cross section, or the dystopian blots in burled wood, or a dragon fruit's Dalmatian-speckled insides. All these things temporize me. It's what Annie Dillard describes in her memoir, *An American Childhood*. Parents who experience pause from "the unnecessary beauty of an ice storm coating trees," while their kids—who "bewilder well," she writes—are simply looking for something to throw. Like when I zone out to cake batter marbling with food coloring in the mixer and my friend's children whom I'm baking with are only concerned with licking the bowl.

Being wowed by fruit or cake batter, I should add, yet fairly sure I'm okay with never seeing the Grand Canyon in person, ought to disqualify me from ever writing about wonder. Then again, maybe that's why I'm drawn to wonder: it pays no attention to priorities.

Before I was old enough to discover it was myth, I assumed goldfish were, over time, the architects of their alleged short-term memory. That they'd tailored their recall to fight the tedious circumference of a fishbowl—preserving their sense of wonder by forgetting they were swimming in circles. No matter how lackluster its surroundings, within seconds, all was new again for a goldfish because it had figured out how to repair its sense of spectacle.

There should be a word for the first listen of a new album that is perhaps not great, but good. It's catchy, carries pathos, is mood modifying. It's destined to hasten you out the door or score your next cab ride as you cross the bridge. It prompts texts after last call. It resuscitates teenage residue and threatens emotional relapse. An album that, upon first listen, discovers a new, hallucinatory wilderness: a pink desert, pewter trees, emerald skies, clouds that sprint by. Or conversely, an album that singes your periphery. What's left is what's in front. Your frame of reference is shot and you are temporarily the most suggestible person alive. An operative.

Is there something to be learned from fast tenderness that wanes just as fast as it forms? Unsophisticated idolatry. A brief devotion to pop songs with nowhere lyrics that repeat one word over and over like a hymn written in neon-tube lighting.

There are movies like that too. So many. Wherein I leave the theater thinking I've just been privy to a masterpiece, and the next day perceive all of its holes, or worse, all of its recycled wiles. I deserve the disappointment. I'm a chump for voice-over and montage, Crewdson-lit suburbs, and all the women in the history of film who've flopped facedown onto beds like possessed slats of wood. I am duped by eye contact in a bar that cuts to the morning after. By odd, intensive but unthinking dance moves that approximate aerobics and clinch, for me, what's charming about a character's nature. I can't help it. Follow shots at a house party, where two tertiary characters are having sex in the bathroom and the lead is a lost boy, barely nodding hellos because he's looking for, not the nearest exit, but the balcony, the girl. These movies in which the characters are so caught up and submerged, they may as well be living underwater where the glow is bleary—where sound gurgles and the world recedes.

Despite everything the movies accomplish, despite these bouts of wonder and alarm, when my heart races, dimples, is weary and deflates, it never exhausts. How is that possible? How does it maintain? Stays going. On and on. It's percussive. It refuses to emote with me because it's uniformly *at it*.

I am—if it's not already clear—disinterested in actually remembering, since I last learned in school, how the heart does what it does. How it pumps blood, carries blood, effects that *lub-dub* sound. I'm in no hurry to understand its inner workings. To wrap my head around how it keeps us alive. To do so would require that I render obsolete all those microscopic people who live inside my heart, for instance. Who blow bubbles into soda and set up homes inside our TVs—seeing what we're seeing, only backward. Who build cozy homes under floorboards. Those guys who, of course, don't exist. Those tiny people who, as a child, I elaborated on in my mind because it was far easier to make sense of how stuff worked if a thumb-sized human was at the helm. These tiny people turned me on to ingenuity— the essence of awe, or at least my relationship to it. They kept the world feasible.

They were, for example, the characters in Mary Norton's *The Borrowers*; a series of books I don't remember reading but on whose illustrated covers I imparted my own stories. If I recall, the Borrowers used matchboxes as kitchen benches, a spool of thread as a chair, a postage stamp as decorative art. The Borrowers were, I made myself believe, living among us: snatching up my spare buttons and re-fashioning them as tabletops or winter sleds. I presumed they made bouquets out of broccoli and laid brick with my brother's Legos, and savored the smell of nail polish just as I did with fresh paint or gasoline. They repurposed our excess was the point.

They experienced the world, I supposed, as I experienced going to the movies: that flash of amazement petitioned, in part, from feeling small in the presence of bigness. In having to arch my neck and fall in with whatever celluloid projection might scoop me up. Like *Fantasia*'s candy-colored bucolic scape. Flirty, fun Centaurettes. The scherzo humor of meddlesome cupids. Pegasus and his family of winged stallions sailing through clouds and diving into crayon waters. A choreography of mushrooms. Of spinning-top bellflowers and heavy-lidded, red, puckered fish. The whole Esther Williams of it all. The ostrich ballet. Like pirouet-ting feather dusters; their paddle feet in fourth position. Or Mickey's broom. How it splintered into a nightmarish army of brooms. How the crash of cymbals, rolling waves, and buckets of water sent me into a panic. *Fantasia* was, in hindsight, my first experience of art's all-overs. Of feel-ing like a casualty to cartoons. Still today, those eight animated segments reify the blunt noise of my childhood anxieties.

There were the characters too. Like Leo's Romeo,

lovesick in a split second. His nose pushed against that fish tank like he'd never seen a real-life Claire Danes.

There was Marisa Tomei's squeak. Her stomp. Her invention. In *My Cousin Vinny*, as if contriving a new hybrid of Bambi from Brooklyn, she pronounced *deer* as *dia*. Tomei as Mona Lisa Vito was a woman with demands who could disqualify you by merely raising the ridge of her brow. Her eyes semaphore. I was mesmerized.

There was the rattling, rotisserie cook of reentry scenes in space movies. There was the Empire State Building: decisive to Romance. Diners: decisive to killers, insomniacs, to fugitives, to prom dates. To Jack Nicholson and his *plain omelet, no potatoes on the plate, a cup of coffee, and a side order of wheat toast.*

There was sex before the camera panned away. Or when the camera panned away: sex.

I'd heard talk of Sharon Stone uncrossing her legs in that infamous interrogation scene, but when I finally saw *Basic Instinct*, it was her shoulders pushed back on the chair that totally stunned me. I'd never experienced shoulders accelerating my pulse. I'd never seen a pair of shoulders communicate point of view. Liquidate a room of all its men and their presumption. Sharon Stone's shoulders pushed back were like *Whoa*.

There was Robin Williams's radius of funny; of voices; of titan warmth. He seemed to outperform humankind. Somehow anthropomorphic, though that makes no sense. As a kid, I believed he was the only person who could be in two places at once. Who, like Genie, could balloon into hot air, float above us, convulse into the cosmos.

Watching movies was consonant to those scenes where the underdog team walks through a stadium tunnel—where their cleats click as light approaches; the blinding pull of sky and turf, and the phenomenon of soon feeling telescoped and giant, both. Watching movies was, and still is, an opportunity for my heart to rush irregularly while the cost, for me, remains low. Because no matter how afflictive, heartbreak on-screen pales in comparison to that first night of a breakup where one's only thought is not *When I wake, I'll be alone*, but *How?* How will I wake up?

There's strength in observing one's miniaturization. That you are insignificant and prone to, and God knows, dumb about a lot. Because doesn't smallness prime us to eventually take up space? For instance, the momentum gained from reading a great book. After *after*, sitting, sleeping, living in its consequence. A book that makes you feel, finally, latched on. Or after *after* we recover from a hike. From seeing fifteenth-century ruins and wondering how Machu Picchu was built when Incans had zero knowledge of the wheel. Smallness can make you feel extra porous. Extra ambitious. Like a small dog carrying an enormous branch clenched in its teeth, as if intimating to the world: *Okay. Where to?*

I remember seeing Etta James live at Salle Wilfrid-Pelletier during the Montreal Jazz Festival, seven or so years before she died. She performed much of the show sitting on a stool, and even then the stage and the theater could not contain her. We the audience, at capacity, fit into her palm. That was the sentiment. Like still air before it becomes a gust of wind. Like water behind a dam; a snowpack before it avalanches. Like Monica Vitti before she sucks on a cigarette, a kettle before it whistles, Etta James, before she performed "At Last," was possibly the most compelling example of potential energy. Ever.

There's might too in the incomplete. In feeling fractional. A failure to carry out is perhaps no failure at all, but rather a minced metric of splendor. The ongoing. The outlawed. The no-patrol. The act of making loose. Of not doing as you've been told. Of betting on miscalculations and cul-de-sacs. Why force conciliation when, from time to time, long-held deep breaths follow what we consider defeat? Why not want a little mania? The shrill of chance, of what's weird. Of purple hats and hiccups. Endurance is a talent that seldom worries about looking good, and abiding has its virtues even when the tongue dries. The intention shouldn't only be to polish what we start but to acknowledge that beginning again and again can possess the acquisitive thrill of a countdown that never reaches zero.

Groping through the dark is, in large part, what writing consists of anyway. Working through and feeling around the shadows of an idea. Getting pricked. Cursing purity. Threshing out. Scuffing up and peeling away. Feral rearranging. Letting form ferment. Letting form pass through you. Observing writing's alp and honoring it by scribbling a whole lot of garbage and then clicking in agreement: *Don't save*. Exaggerating until it hurts. Until you limp and are forced to rest, and then say what you mean to the sound of thunder's cannonade; to the lilting hum of ghosts that only haunt the sea, or of Debussy in your earbuds, and the sometimes-style of piano that sounds pleasantly soiree-drunk and stumbly.

Until you write what is detectable but dislodges you. Like the smell of cinnamon. Like sex with someone where your bodies conform, and your hands and legs fold into each other, even if it's been years. Even if there's been hate and pitiless hurt.

Thinking of someone the way he was is really just another way of writing. Thinking about someone I was once in love with—how he'd peel an orange and hand me a slice or how his white T-shirt would peek out from under his gray sweatshirt. The way it would curve around his neck somehow made me disposed to him. Thinking about that crescent of white cotton is a version of writing. Thinking about how, once, to make me less nervous before an interview I was preparing for, he pulled his pants down in public. Remembering his smile as my nerves relaxed, and as he pulled his pants up and looked around, is how I write and what I write about, even if it's nothing I've ever written about.

My quick-summoned first love—how everything was enough because I knew so little but felt cramped with certainty—is, I'm afraid, just like writing. That is to say, what can transpire if writing becomes a reason for living outside the real without prying it open. How, like first love, writing can be foiling, agitated, totally addictive. Sweet, insistent, jeweled. Consuming though rarely nourishing. A new tactility.

First love fools you into thinking about nothing else. Into believing a whole city belongs to you; that you can conquer . . . it doesn't matter what. Which is, experientially speaking, furthest from finding yourself. Which, let's face it: can be temporarily curative. Time off. Rescue. A beer. Its froth. Thinking maybe it'd be good to travel. To go to Budapest and pick fights in Budapest, and then make up over a game of Twenty Questions on the bus from Budapest to Vienna.

First love is all sensation and ambient zooms, and letting the world ebb. Like writing, occasionally, it feels combustive. Greedy. It's unsophisticated and coaxes you into making promises about the far future and imbibing the moment. Into growing gullible fast, frantically so, and forgetting about yourself—about your exception. Writing does the same. It lays siege.

Because writing is, off and on, running smack into *Aha!* and staring down *Duh*. Is my function to reach zero and leave nothing in the way of obstructing truth? Or to tender what's still shapeless? The baggy fit of feelings before they've found their purpose. How can I present what's, for now, finished, while also taking comfort in knowing it will evolve? That these words are only materials; provisions for keeping me observant and hopefully light-footed enough to plan my next project. My next many.

Which is why the mode for labeling a visual artist's work, when exhibited, has always appealed to me. How the artist's name and the title of the piece are followed by the medium.

- Oil on canvas
- Tape and acrylic on panel
- Plywood, forged iron, plaster, latex paint, twine
- Wood, beeswax, leather, fabric, and human hair
- Living artist, glass, steel, mattress, pillow, linen, water, and spectacles
- Fat, felt, and cardboard box in metal and glass display case
- Bronze
- Metal and plastic
- Hand-spun wool
- Fabric collage
- Carrara marble and teakwood base
- Red pigment and varnish on paper
- Video, black-and-white, sound
- Dyed cotton, grommets, rope, and thread, in two parts

I find the plainness and economizing record of materials handled calming. Realistic yet not austere, because what corresponds—the words *oil on canvas*—has everything and nothing to do with what I'm looking at. The disconnect wakes me up. The words *plywood*, *plaster*, and *twine* are deadpan and even grim. *Bronze* is bodily and somehow lewd. Characterizing a video installation as having "sound" seems like, for whatever reason, a breakthrough. That a glass display case or teakwood base is principle to the piece feels hospitable. "Fabric collage" is pseudonymous.

Too bad this sort of reduction cannot be achieved with books. Tables of contents don't even come close. Indexes, maybe.

Because writing is a grunt, and when it's good, writing is body language. It's a woman narrowing her eyes to express incredulity. It's an elbow propped on the edge of a table when you're wrapping up an argument, or to signify you're just getting started. An elbow propped on the edge of a table is an adverb.

I've heard rumors that writing can feel glamorous. But only glamorous, I'd guess, in the way a stretch limo might feel glamorous. No matter the pomp, one still has to crouch inside. Like skulking through a low-lit leather tunnel. An uncooperative space. Writing is awkward work and it's become clearer to me why friends of mine have relinquished their desks and write instead from the comfort of their beds. Not in bed. From bed. Like sea otters floating on their backs, double-chinned and banging their front paws on a keyboard.

It's imperative that writing consists of not living up to

your own taste. Of leaving the world behind so you can hold fast to what's strange inside; what's unlit. A soreness. A neglected joy. The way forward is perhaps not maintaining a standard for accuracy but appraising what naturally heaps.

Writing is losing focus and winning it back, only to lose it once more. Hanging on despite the nausea of producing nothing good by noon, despite the Sisyphean task of arriving at a conclusion that pleases. The spiteful blink of my cursor: how it mocks. The rude temptation of a crisp day: how it bullies. Writing will never be as satisfying as observing someone whom I knew was terrible get caught in an embarrassing lie; as satisfying as the *pop!* I anticipate when twisting open a Martinelli's apple juice or when I pour hot coffee over ice come summer or lace up skates in the winter—the firm tug of hooking the top part of the boot. Writing is a closed pistachio shell.

And yet, despite claims, no writer hopes for ideas to take complete shape. Approximation is the mark. Many times, writing that clinches lacks incandescence—the embers have cooled. A need for completeness can, off and on, squander cadence. Isn't it fun to read a sentence that races ahead of itself? That has the effect of stopping short—of dirt and cutaway rocks tumbling down the edge of a cliff, alerting you to the drop. As the critic, author, and poet Clive James wrote of Proust's *À la recherche du temps perdu*: "It reminds me of a sandcastle that the tide reached before its obsessed constructor could finish it; but he knew that would happen, or else why build it on a beach?"

What I enjoy is this. Responding to an artist's work as if it were a missive. A film can be a fling I'll cool with sentences I address to the director but that I'll tuck into this essay instead. I've written to Akerman, Leos Carax, Antonioni, to Douglas Sirk's Technicolor; his sylvan winters and obscene display of periwinkle. Love letters, generally. Essays that do not concern these directors' works but are addressed to them—in spirit, tone, wash—because these directors have, over time, caused me to bend into shape visions that were long hibernating. How Agnès Varda, for example, introduced me to women with implication. How Varda portrays the defamed—often women—as irrepressible and in control of a mind built for maneuvering beyond convention. These women who perhaps even balk at the word *survival* and favor instead a far more fluctuant current: *continuance*.

I've written as well to Bresson, Bergman, Rohmer's girls, Rivette, John Huston because I'll never get over Susan Tyrrell's Oma in *Fat City*. Her boozy pout is a wreck no one recuperates from. She is unconcealed. Her dress's back zipper unzipping. Her wail: both mother and child in labor.

There's no use in trying to bounce back from first seeing Giulietta Masina in *La Strada*. Her globe face is somehow panoramic: a pendant, the highest wattage, "an artichoke." The sort of face one writes to because Masina was the queen of the encounter. Watching her means paying attention.

I've written to Mazursky and Cassavetes and their women sick with an itch, dissatisfied to the point of dancing alone in their homes to music that isn't so much music but dull pain with a tune. Women with demands that are mysterious even to themselves. Women who are runaways in their own kitchens. Women who are in no rush to respond to a world that's only conceived them as its consequence. Who experience deep movement by playing air piano. Who are wind-oriented. Who are Gena Rowlands. Who are Jill Clayburgh—bearably, unbearably, lugging a big canvas down the street, alone. These women who brilliantly source endings for takeoff.

I've written to Claire Denis, Maren Ade, to James Gray's New York, to Mia Hansen-Løve's yearning boyish-girlish unease. To her films as photo albums. To her regard for a person's things. I've written to Abbas Kiarostami's ballads. His least possible, spare approach to poetry and splayed views that above all are an indication of the times as they weigh on country and personhood, and how the two are prodigiously connected. I'll send notes, again and again, to Wong Kar-wai. To Wim Wenders and his roads, and those questions that can only occur in cars. To Maya Deren! To Jane Campion! Andrea Arnold! Desplechin! I write to him a lot. To Satyajit Ray, whose character Durga, the mischievous daughter and Apu's sister in *Pather Panchali*, is my namesake. Ray once said in an interview that he directs his films "in harmony with the rhythm of human breathing." I've tried writing with that belief in mind, discovering instead how deep inhales and the release of a strong exhale are furthest from writing's doubled-up glove. Moving pictures are a better match for that kind of subliminal flight.

There are days when I can't push through my frustrations unless I write to Barbara Loden's Wanda. To that last shot when the camera freezes on the wilt of her face. She is all at once unused but *oh,* so used up. Or very used *to.* Why is it that when a woman is occupied by the voice in her head, or the wear of her day, or the landscape that passes through her eyes like windows on a train, the world assumes she is up for grabs? A vacant stare does not mean vacancy. It's the inverse of invitation, and yet.

Other times, the art becomes a condition—incredibly fitting. At first glance, my friend Sarah *is* a Cy Twombly; her favorite painter. She speaks in scratches, keeps dead flowers for weeks. Her thoughts are erratic, sarcastic, rascally. Her lips dark amaranth. Ordinarily, her makeup appears out of focus and, as a matter of course, slightly marked up. Rose-*ish.* Soft with contempt, as if she'd rather her blush stain than blush. Mid-consideration, Sarah will pause, shake her head, and smudge two ideas. To punctuate what she believes to be true, she'll raise her index finger as if penciling the air with her talon nail. In her wake, the room drips. Like Cy, there is a touch of the unfinished with Sarah: what's fraying could be trimmings. Like Cy, where crayon on canvas is so much more than "scrawl"—twenty-one feet of it that requires two hydraulic lifts to install—there are times when my friendship with Sarah invites remove. Stand too close, for too long, and the lines muddy. At any rate, isn't it lovely to, once in a while, feel small in the presence of your friend? Awed. Fortunate to experience nearness that calls upon space.

Because there is trust too, in feeling small. The letting-in that comes from letting go. Gazing up at the taut tract of cables on a suspension bridge and never worrying *Will this hold?* Or shooting up an elevator, seventy-four stories high, without feeling much until the doors slide open and you encounter a south-facing view and the precarious pull of a pane of glass.

Nudging my mother's eldest sister for details while she tells me a story about my grandparents. This too gauges smallness. The muscle that builds from yielding to my aunt Jennifer's decades, to the scalloped edges of her memory, reacquaints me to my most atomic self: where I come from. Even when I was nothing, I was arriving.

This Christmas, Jennifer recorded a story about her parents for all the grandchildren on my mom's side to keep forever. She titled it "Such Fine Parents." The insistence of "Such" is not merely avowal, but love distinguished. She typed out the story and printed copies. She punched holes in each page and placed them one by one in red folders. I received mine in the mail and hurried to read it, only to be slowed down by tears every few sentences. The pull of ancestry. How without stint I could love someone I will never meet: my maternal grandmother. She died when my mother was fourteen years old. I was born sixteen years later, to the day.

Reading about my grandfather Felix, courting my grandmother Dulcie, how he'd ride his Harley-Davidson—"sold off by the departing foreign troops," Jennifer noted—from Calcutta to the French-colonized Chandannagar, where Dulcie was teaching at St. Joseph's Convent, was like reading my past, the fiction of those years before I was born, before my mother and her two sisters were born, and have it beam bright and, more critically, become document. I've heard the stories. I've read my mother's words too, about Felix's furniture business, about Dulcie's fondness for dancing despite being considered a prudish young woman, but for some reason now—as it can only happen in time—my aunt Jennifer's telling of it flickered on the page. Like the Hooghly River's "silvering" moonlight that accompanied Dulcie and Felix on their walks before they were husband and wife, never holding hands but prolonging their time spent together on the way back to the convent by "slowing their steps," my aunt wrote, "as the gates to the school loomed large." Romance's silhouette as it's been recounted to me, the stalling tactics of courtship between Felix and Dulcie, resides in my circuitry.

Rewinding two generations and picturing my grandparents before they were even parents is like watching fireworks backward: tinsel swallowed into the night sky instead of spitting out from it. Undoing time for a moment and expunging myself from the record is, strangely, confirmation of my lowercase history. A remembrance of what's impossible to remember. A sixth sense I've long guessed is special to those who are born with leftover matter ferrying them rearward. We're the type who ask too many questions—an irritating amount, really. But who ask without claim or exigency. The want is the want and it goes on like that. My prelude was a waltz Dulcie loved to dance. She and Felix *then*, are like Etta James in concert: potential energy.

On January 8, 1947, they were married. Morning Mass followed by a wedding breakfast, and later, a party. Dulcie's dress was cut, my mother once told me, from postwar parachute silk. *It's what was available at the time.* In the only photograph I've seen from that day, the newly married couple's smile looks ten seconds gone from original mirth. As if the moment has lapsed and the marriage has begun. Dulcie's white-gloved hand is tucked inside Felix's elbow so elegantly that conjured quick in my mind are replicas of her hands everywhere: pawing piano keys, buffing brass, folding a handkerchief on its diagonal just so. Steadying her grip on a steel banister as Schroeder, their Labrador, lovingly shoves himself between her legs. Hands like Dulcie's—long fingers that form a low mountain range from simply resting on the edge of a table—are unmistakable. As with nearly all elegant things, they photograph eerie. The way a rose stem looks arthritic.

In that same photograph, Felix stands tall, square, and sturdy, wearing his pin-striped suit—the lapels wide. Occasionally my mind wanders to that suit and I'll consider what happened to it. Where is it hanging? Was it folded into a box? Where do wedding suits end up? Was it given away or did it outlive my grandfather like how a favorite reading chair might outlive its person? The sallow tuft of its seat, eternally styled just for one. Tailored pant legs on anyone else become costume: roomy chutes, flaccid, or goofy and squat. I'll see old men on the street shrinking into their clothes—trousers girded around mini guts, jacket shoulders too stubborn to sag—and I'll think about my grandfather.

He was a large man whom I only met once, when I was three years old, visiting Calcutta for the first time. I have no memory of the trip, though of course I do. I have unintelligible copy. Recall the texture of chiffon. I have the impression of a city, of looking down just in time to skip over a puddle. The sustained toot of car horns. Of bare lightbulbs hanging above fruit stalls at night and sun halos flecking my vision from having peered up at palm trees, absorbed by how they siphon blue sky through their plumed leaves. While I've been back to visit over the years, that first trip is, I wonder, when my memory switched into gear. When I began to pile experiences, grafting them without motive— suddenly hyperaware of the cone-shaped hats on the clown pattern on my two-piece pajamas, or how making eye contact with a stranger could seal that stranger's face in my mind. How now I have at my disposal a whole catalog of strangers' faces, for no reason at all.

One image in particular from my first time in Calcutta comes to mind: of me and my cousins, barely clothed, enjoying the hell out of pretend-coiffing Felix's hair. He's sitting shirtless at the massive teak kitchen table, noble as ever in an imaginary salon. We're jumping up and down and standing on our tiptoes, pinching plastic clips into his hair. It's possible I've been described this episode or that it exists more readily as a photograph conspiring to reshuffle my clarity. Like when I use someone else's keyboard—the letter E is jammed; the space bar's lost its spring. Or how a cover of a familiar song usually forces further consideration before I can identify it. How, all at once, what I know for sure— the words to a damn song—can feel frustratingly just out of reach.

There's no use in trying to figure out which came first, my memory of the hair clips in that Calcutta kitchen or my mother's telling of that afternoon nearly three decades ago. I've come around to the conciliatory quality of untruths. Memory fans out from imagination, and vice versa, and why not. Memory isn't a well but an offshoot. It goes secretly. Comes apart. Deceives. It's guilty of repurposing the meaning of deep meaning and poking fun at what you've emotionalized.

And besides, it feels more covert to have no evidence. To believe that something you've experienced will build on your extent—your extent as a person who sees things, and is moved by things—without ever having to prove those things happened exactly as they happened. Substantiating is grueling, monotonous. It's what life expects of you. Memory is trust open to doubt.

Perhaps they weren't hair clips but clothespins. Who knows. We were children. Recycled containers were toys. Fonts on cereal boxes provided an exciting new style for drawing the hanging loop of a lowercase *g*. I played house because keeping busy looked entertaining. The hectic woman was a character in a video game, reaching the next level. Her unavailable stare as she opened and closed cabinets while listening to a child's tedious story, or, by instinct, sponging the sink's grime while talking on the phone strangely appealed to me. Perhaps it's because, as a child, I perceived responsibilities as possibilities, carrying around one of those Sealtest bags of 2 percent milk, pretending it was my baby and returning it to the fridge before it got warm.

To this day, watching a woman mindlessly tend to one thing while doing something else absorbs me. Like securing the backs of her earrings while wiggling her feet into her shoes. Like staring into some middle distance, where lines soften, and where she separates the relevant from the immaterial. A woman carries her inner life—lugs it around or holds it in like fumes that both poison and bless her—while nourishing another's inner life, many others actually, while never revealing too much madness, or, possibly, never revealing where she stores it: her island of lost mind. Every woman has one. And every woman grins when the question is asked, *What three items would you bring to a desert island?* Because every woman's been, by this time, half living there.

What other imaginations decked my childhood? Riches I perceived simply from staring long enough at something plain, and in staring long enough, I was recasting it. At Christmas, the tin of Quality Street chocolates had the allure of, not hidden treasure exactly, but close. Cellophane has that effect. Little wrapped jewels that came with a map I studied close. Purple twist=Hazelnut Caramel. Green=Milk Choc Block. Pink=Fudge. Nobody ate the Toffee Penny. They outlasted the holidays entirely. Even today when I see the nugget-shaped toffees, I'm reminded of how blank those days that followed Christmas and New Year's felt. How now I often regret not being tucked into bed before midnight on December 31.

A Bruegel print hanging in our home was essentially my jackpot. I mined that peasant-wedding scene so intently that elements of its narrative details, like porridge bowls, the lip of a jug, that pureed Bruegel red—like tomato soup from the can—and a child in the foreground licking a plate, all belong to my memory's reel. It's the merging that occurs from housing a mental archive instead of contending with the sound of parents who were speaking to each other in a strained tone. Of momentarily acquitting myself of childhood grievances: of all the birds we hear in trees but never see, but know are there.

Rarely shelved in our home was a copy of Edward Said's *Orientalism*. Some books were just left out like that. No reason, no mind. The mess drove my father mad. I stared at the book's cover, watching it fade over the course of one summer, where it sat on the edge of a table in a particularly sunlit room. Either the dining room or the living room, the same year new curtains were being sewn at the tailor's with fabric my mother had brought back from a recent trip to Calcutta. The book's cover features a painting by the nineteenth-century artist Jean-Léone Gérôme titled *The Snake Charmer.* A blue-tiled wall, an audience of armed men, a fipple flute player, and a naked boy whose back is to us. A large, thick snake is coiled around the boy's muscular body. I remember the boy's bum. It looked real; round like melons. I was only slightly scandalized by the painting because I couldn't understand why the boy was naked. I somehow knew it was intentionally plotting intrigue. The West's fascination with the East. I knew this, but I didn't. The notion was vague. A sentiment I'd heard expressed at home and one that wallpapered our bookshelves—the bindings of academic tomes, somehow bolder than fiction. Isn't it curious how some fonts appear more dogmatic than others? How italicized neon pink on a book of nonfiction is suddenly: *Commentary!* Sometimes I think our house was too full of ideas, near choked by them. Other days I'm grateful ours was a house of unrest, because isn't that what ideas are?

It was a house where adults came and went: for meetings; for tea; to discuss, to organize, to speak with their hands; to flex histrionically about history. My father's theater group or the South Asian women's center my mother cofounded. Potlucks. Dinners. My parents had built a home, and continued to build their separate homes later, where ideas circuited the space, and where I gathered what I could or, rather, what I cared for, like the round shape of that boy's bum on the cover of Edward Said's *Orientalism*. At any rate, comprehension was a series of clues. *The Snake Charmer*'s whole scene looked precarious because it didn't seem like a painting but a photograph. Rarely does a subject disturb me as much as when it slopes my ability to discern what's real and what isn't. Likely because I fear—more alarmingly quick as years pass—the fine line between being conscious and becoming jaded.

I've been so young for so long and so old for longer—so heart-wrinkled and naive all at once. So brow-furrowed but heart-open too; a detective. Snooping yet easily sidetracked. I'll believe anything because I want to understand, yet understanding can sometimes organize itself like a series of false starts.

It's part of what happens when you develop an optimism that wasn't inherited, necessarily. An American optimism. A Canadian one. A pop-culturally American one. A North American one. A TV optimism. However you like to delineate your geographies. It's an optimism of remove. Of untying myself from my parents' lives by becoming enthusiastic—at times forcefully—about my own. The con-artistry that first-generation kids learn young: to adapt, yet remain amenable to your home. To identify how seamlessly the world expects you to adapt and, as a result, how early you practice pushback. You are born spinning. In dispute. I was my own project.

But memorizing the Bruegel or the cover of Said's book was part of my practice formed early to repossess. Or to confuse repossession with the distraction it allowed. Zero-ing in and slingshotting far were tantamount. For a girl so alert, I was absent. For a girl so AWOL, my insides were a microcosm of raw materials. Or rising sea levels. It really could be either. It's as though I miscarried all that glee we are entitled to in childhood. At picnics, I was impatient to wipe the sticky off my fingers. Honeydew was a drag.

Because ever since I can remember, I've been captivated by life's second ply. The sharks inside the sandbox. The horror of seeing faces everywhere. On electric outlets. In food. Or how daylight looks curiously divine when it shines underground through subway grates. Or the woman con-firmed by her superstitions, who says little and wears sun-glasses indoors; who attracts attention like a big house set back on its overgrown lawn.

Moreover, life's second ply meant envisioning with enough detail, for example, the DJ whose voice seemed to grow out from the radio each morning. Based on how she spoke, I decided she had a fondness for long-haired cats.

For French manicures, a glossy lip, and glittered eye shadow. Her face twinkling—communicating at all times—even when she was silent. Makeup as Morse code.

Pip's eloping understanding of the world; that too is an example of life's second ply. How on the first page of *Great Expectations*, he imagines his dead parents, whom he never met: "My first fancies regarding what they were like were unreasonably derived from their tombstones. The shape of the letters on my father's gave me an odd idea that he was a square, stout, dark man with curly black hair."

Like Pip, *my first most vivid and broad impression of the identity of things* may as well have occurred in a marsh. On an inclement beach where the sky is broth and gusts of wind flare up like shameless hints. Similar to Pip, I might miss the big ideas. I'll devise another layer to avoid what's at stake. I care little for plot and prefer a lingering glow, and often flip back a few pages because I overlooked a crucial turn while half reading on the train, distracted by a group of French teenagers who are, by some chemical law or cultural precedent, cooler than I'll ever be.

Increasingly, I find it hard to read on the train. My mind roams off the page, and no matter what novel I'm reading, I'll angle instead for its less essential stories; the ones I raffle might spout hope or an image I can more readily hold on to. Like the burnt-cork mustaches Sonya and Natasha paint on their faces at Christmas; that they wear as costumes to the widow Melyukov's party. The burnt-cork mustaches that Sonya and Natasha don't bother wiping off before bed, lying awake for a long time, as Tolstoy wrote, simply "talking about their happiness." What comes to mind when I think of *War and Peace* is the moonlit sleigh ride on Christmas Eve. The frosty air. Sonya's fur coat. The earth speeding past and the "magical kingdom" that Nikolai perceives. The kiss that smelled of burnt cork.

There are times when the degree to which *I just don't want to know* manifests in, recently, overhearing a man on his phone say to whoever was on the other end, "There's no proper way to say this." The man was standing next to me on the corner of West Thirteenth, and because I couldn't bear to overhear what his next words would be, I dashed across Seventh Avenue, leaving behind a perfectly warm patch of sunlight. As cars zoomed past between us, I looked back at him. He was not so much pacing but pivoting on the ball of his foot like someone who was now patiently at the mercy of another person's reaction. I bought a small bag of grapes from a fruit stand and started eating them, tasting the filmy dirt-wax of unwashed grapes; pleased that I'll never know what that man owned up to. That his privacy belonged to him was less an indication of my courtesy and more a combination of other factors. The mystery! Obviously. Judgment too stirs my imagination. It's awful, but there's nothing like arbitrary judgment to reposition how badly I might be feeling; how, briefly, a stranger's drama can recirculate the air.

There's also the sheer unfeasibility of overhearing as much as one does in a city so dense as New York, without a break—without the truce of silence. Even in elevators you can still hear car sirens. At home, the neighbors are fighting.

I'm fairly confident my compulsion for stockpiling has kept me at a distance from possessing answers to my own questions. I suspend them—the questions, that is—in my writing. I ignore them like I ignore the incessant drip of my leaky faucet; putting on my headphones and turning up the volume. I ignore them like someone who goes to sleep in her bed but hopes to wake up—still in her bed, but in a field with only the clean range of anonymous field in view. As if the field was on another planet where the flora is familiar-*ish*. Earth-*ish*. Blades of grass–*ish*. The breeze, occasional. Where every sound is contained; nothing incoming or fleeing. A sanctuary for my one mode of being that has no name other than it exists as some substratum of myself, from which images emerge and come into sight unannounced. It's there that the commotion begins. The quietist riot, at first. What's irrepressible shoots up, and all of a sudden I am life-driven, numb and tingly. Opulent and part velocity. I am on the move and spared another day of panic; of feeling outdistanced. All of a sudden the words are meant. On the loose, but meant. I am individualized. I have my own attention.

How many versions of happiness involve a smile? Are determined by feeling fulfilled? How many versions of happiness require acquisition? My version swears by distraction. By curling up inside the bends of parentheses. I digress, but not idiomatically. I digress intentionally. This piece, for example, is largely composed of interceptions. Starting somewhere, ending elsewhere. Testing the obnoxious reach of my tangents. Likely failing. While I rely, perhaps in excess, on my wad of massed-together nostalgia and unrelated brain waves, my hope is that there is in fact a frame. That conjunctions are accomplice. That awareness isn't merely a stopgap; that it develops beyond a tally. How a stranger's laundry line discloses the arrival of a newborn or the week's absentmindedness: once-white sheets and T-shirts, all flapping in the wind, all tinted pink. And how for some, to-do lists are indiscriminate and often unintelligible. *Un*-poems:

1. Toothpaste
2. Advil
3. Coriander
4. Shirley . . . Last name?
5. Dried apricots, feta
6. Dinner with Collier
7. Steel wool
8. Find an alternate
9. Email Jonathan
10. Tell Lucy about Lucy, the cream poodle on West 11th with hip dysplasia
11. Consider Halifax; a yellow lampshade

12. A low heel
13. Return her Hardwick, her sequins
14. Walk to the water
15. Don't forget the pie!!
16. Coconut milk
17. Tell Mama
18. Tomatoes

It's true too that in childhood fending off the need to adhere was easier if I devised my own rhythm. Whatever I could drum was a drum. Mixing spoons were mics, though I was too shy to sing louder than a hum. Even today, no matter how simple the tune, I'll ruin it. The tricky jump of "Happy Birthday" continues to give me trouble.

Power line transmission towers were giants guarding the dry, somewhat planetary, outskirts of what lies just beyond city limits. Dal was a moat on my plate of rice. Salt and pepper shakers were united in holy matrimony. I thought David Bowie was Dracula. And Lou Reed was Frankenstein's monster. I didn't *really*. But I didn't *not*, either.

And my grandfather Felix was—for one day in Calcutta—my life-sized doll. I hope it was clothespins we were pinching into his hair. Like little soldiers at attention on his head. I've never heard a recording of my voice as a kid, but I'd guess my giggle was full of spit, and just a bit carried away.

That first trip to India is blotchy, untidy. Only floret-sized memories bloom. Because unbeknownst to me, I was familiarizing myself with the lineal estate of where I'm from—with the premium of being a jet-lagged three-year-old who was too occupied by the advent of cousins to remember to close the mosquito net in the bed I shared with my mother and brother whenever I'd sneak out in the early morning and play with a bootleg Mickey Mouse toy. He had green ears. His painted eyes looked strung out. Everything there was the same but different. A good lesson to learn very young.

In my aunt Jennifer's telling of "Such Fine Parents," she calls Felix and Dulcie "Mummy and Daddy." Over the phone, at nearly seventy, she still says Mummy and Daddy. There's a salvaging property to her tone as though my aunt is recovering her first self: daughterhood. When the world was demarcated by two parents and two sisters and a bird menagerie on the veranda. When the act of wanting was, my mother recounted to me, the burning desire for bell-bottom jeans. Like the ones she'd seen in American *Vogue* while flipping through the pages, listening to the Supremes.

For Easter this year, Jennifer and my mother are taking the train from Montreal to Toronto to visit Lois, their middle sister. It's her birthday. Whenever the three Chew sisters are together—three sets of round cheeks cushioning the bottom frame of three pairs of glasses—I imagine them making great riches from speaking in old sayings and chattering about nothing in particular, such as a cardigan that was on sale. I imagine them laughing until the air around them bends. I imagine them sitting on a couch, crossing their legs at their ankles, wearing the slippers they bring with them everywhere.

I imagine them young again too. Having not yet crossed the Atlantic, living in their Elliot Road flat; a short walk from Loreto House, where my mother went to school. I imagine them going to the tailor. Wearing cat-eye glasses. Attempting the absurd: to coordinate three smiles in one photo. I imagine them eating hot cross buns and, later, accompanying Felix to the butcher and begging him to save the doomed fate of two ducks, and returning home with pets that now waddle up the stairs.

I've long perceived sisterhood as a secret inlet. A relationship whose shape is uniquely undisclosed. As though the world shrinks into a nucleus formed of borrowed clothes and ordained fights, matching prepubescent limbs and terrible haircuts; one sister's nose invariably more aquiline than the others'. One sister noticeably more dawdling than the others—picking flowers, not combing her hair. Getting sick on her birthday.

Does the discrete viability of sisterhood rise since birth, sharing a heart like you might share speech patterns? Like a tin-can telephone, but for the voice in your head. As if you have an innate fluency for sharing the blanket so that everyone's toes are covered. In childhood, having a sister, especially if she was older, meant sharing a wall with—it's possible—some likeness of your near-future self. Movies, books, the March sisters, all of it, devised a rubric that engrossed me because sisterhood amounted to what I envied: not having to learn how to join. You were already part of something. You could be a crowd. You could troop places. You could be recruited the way a pop song recruits you. You could link arms. Your crowd was loud. You could be the quiet one couched inside the crowd, nodding off to the sound of sisters sneaking in one last burst of energy before bed. You could develop a dramatic flair for fighting. A penchant for doing nothing except to sit in the company of a girl and her mirror; a girl and her closet; a girl and the leeching shame of a mistake she believes makes her undeserving of anything.

You could witness coming-of-age as it revealed itself between a sister and your parents. You could have someone magically absorb whatever terror was compassing your week by lending you her jacket. By saying, "Keep it." You could have an adjunct mother who braided your hair differently from how your mother braided your hair. You could admire the manner in which your sister establishes herself outside the home; how it was possible to escape the madness that closes in on you from being a daughter with gratitude, but also a daughter who is desperate to slide the ribbon out from her hair and race toward heartbreak; pacifying that initial lacking with, it turns out, even more lacking.

While this isn't the case with all sisters, with some, when they reunite even for a short visit, the whole world is suddenly younger. An atmosphere of holiday is established:

someone suggests a snack right before dinner, and newly received wisdom substantiates an old argument. Everyone drops the possessive "my," and grown women start talking about Mom and Dad this, Mom and Dad that. When sisters walk side by side, they move slow and talk speedy, and seem somehow capable of time travel. Or perhaps sisterhood is, plainly, a version of time travel.

No matter where I am, when the Chew sisters are together, like Easter weekend in Toronto, I am emotionally solvent. I feel a sense of alcove. I think of the painter Amrita Sher-Gil's *Three Girls*, a print my mother framed and gave to Jennifer and Lois many years ago. Like the Bruegel, I know it well. Three girls in salwar kurtas—orange, mint, red—form a corner. As though painted by candlelight, it has an orblike quality. Solemn, no one is smiling. I'm fond of the Sher-Gil because I know it spoke to my mother's earliest framework. How her context since birth has been "the youngest of three." The last one to experience her firsts.

When your mother is the baby of her family—when that expression's been used to lovingly characterize her rank—she shrinks before you, covering her eyes when the MGM lion roars. Socks sliding down her ankles and bunching on the brim of her loafers. She's focused on a mosquito bite; scratching it until it welts and bleeds. Her voice is higher. It might crack when she asks questions about the fit of things. How the cherry liqueur gets inside the chocolate and if it's possible to sit on clouds.

My mother has another Sher-Gil print hanging at hers, in the living room above the large Chinese chest we've owned for as long as I can remember. Carved into the dark wood is a panorama of flowers, a pavilion, a bridge, some people and pines. Too much story whittled into its wood for me to have ever endowed my own. I used to dig dust from its grooves and smell the metal tang of brass on my fingers after playing with its latch. My mother stores blankets inside the chest. Or old clothes she never wears. Or stuff belonging to my father. I once fished from its contents a pilled Cardinals baseball tee and a paper-thin, plaid shirt with snap buttons. Both were his from the seventies when he was a student at Washington University. I know this because of a picture I found that I keep in a folder of other photos. In the picture, my father's hair is long and his glasses are tinted. He's skinny but looks strong. Like he hasn't yet become the father I know who dwells. Who, when arguing, espouses his point by taking a deep breath and saying, "Look, in the final analysis . . ."

When I put on the plaid shirt, at home in my own apartment, pulling my arm through each sleeve, I smell the Chinese storage chest that sits under the Sher-Gil in my mother's upper duplex on Coolbrook Avenue in Montreal. Its bitter camphor odor is the first smell I understood as combative. More than merely attributive, it repelled moths. Those papery phantom pests I used to fear but now don't mind. Ladybugs, on the other hand . . .

It's possible too that the shirt smells like my father in

his twenties. The notion of him. He's on a walk with a friend, somewhere near St. Louis, posing for a picture alongside a creek; finding his balance on slippery rocks. Maybe he was tossing smooth pebbles as if making use of what's bottled up. Anticipating the plop. Maybe my father had a great arm and could throw far. Come to think of it, I've never seen him throw anything, not even a ball. I've known him to be hunched over things: papers, his phone, toweling dry our dog, deliberating between pounds of chicken at the grocery store, sitting on the foot of his bed and staring off course between putting on socks, or sitting across from his record player with his head bowed, listening to Sonny Rollins, Linton Kwesi Johnson, Dave Brubeck's airy stalling tactics.

On vacations, my father will retreat to where the view is less crowded, as if in defiance of all tourists, everywhere. He'll lean his body on a guardrail at a museum and look down at all the foot traffic instead of at the paintings. He'll later describe to me the stout carriage of one security guard; how her *Not having it* attitude was more compelling than any of the art.

The shirt smells like my Baba before he was a father. Before he had a baby boy who'd shake his diapered bum to the Bronski Beat. And soon after: me. His daughter whom he calls "the girl," to whom he's passed on a reflex for absence. The shirt smells like what I can only describe as *a stretch*. Those years when you are responsible only for yourself and develop, as a result, a potent sense of anonymity, despite combing the days for purpose. When, briefly, nothing is catastrophic though everything feels precisely gut-poignant, and falling asleep comes easy, and you're still not sure where to look when smiling. And isn't that nice?

It smells like those years, between 1973 and 1977, when my father, for a period, was living with his roommate Bruce, painting houses in the summer and working at a jazz club where, one night he manned the lights for Gerry Mulligan and, another time, Charles Mingus. The shirt smells like paint drying and the sound of Mingus's hard bop, and while it smells like none of those things, it does. In remembering to forget—which is altogether different from forgetting—I've picked up other tendencies. Like unlearning in general, but also, I've trained my ears to sniff out trails. I've trained my nose to interpret sounds. Smells conjure scenes from movies, for example. Basically, and for what it's worth—not much!—I'm proficient at having my attention drawn away. I've adjusted my senses to life's incoherence. The sweet whiff of gasoline is Tippi Hedren clutching her cheeks as cars explode and birds circle on high; is Angela Bassett walking away while the white BMW burns.

There was a period in college when the sound of photocopiers in my library's basement was, I'm uncertain why: *blue*. Perhaps their ceaselessness reminded me of waves. Paralleling the surf and sway, and roll, on loop. Paper shooting out the tray like lapping ocean water foaming on the beach.

Putty brown is, forever, Faye Dunaway's edged enunciation of "Ecumenical Liberation Army," because isn't that whole movie various shades of putty brown? The smell of clementine peels on my fingertips at Christmas is Nat King Cole's confiding baritone. Sarah Vaughan singing "Lullaby of Birdland" feels like the touch of worn cotton; a rotation of old T-shirts my mother wears when she's cooking, listening to jazz compilations, snapping her fingers as Vaughan's voice elegantly ladles the words "weepy old willow."

And when I hear Mingus's "Goodbye Pork Pie Hat"—that pendulous elegy, sad but sleuthing, like a gloomy gumshoe's anthem—I smell my father's plaid shirt. Its collar has since lost its stiff. One button snaps with less *snap!* It hangs in my closet in Brooklyn, sharing a hanger with two other shirts—an indignity I should fix.

There are so many photos I've never seen and questions I do not ask, because seeing them and asking them, I worry, precipitates an end. The difference between collection and memorial has, in recent years, become less clear to me. My instinct to write things down often feels like obituary. And with my parents, a gratuitous gamble with time.

Will I regret not soliciting details about their trip to Nicaragua? The red dress. That straw hat. Yes and no. There are, as ever, the tokens that provide a layout of my parents' thinking; how they've never ceased to interrogate the world and how narrative, as a practice, oils their rationale.

I grew up in a house of stories. The good fortune of having parents who moved away young from their parents—from their initial understanding of the world—but never completely. Who speak in layers and have held, each in his and her way, a belief that symbolism can gel life's experiences. Can inspire material or an event to get passed down.

Like my brother's middle name: Sandino. It was winter 1984. My mother was six months pregnant when they visited Nicaragua. In pictures, she is growing out her perm and three months shy of becoming a mother for the first time. She was then, I wonder, a boiled-down combination of cluelessness and fear, prospect, pleasure, thick doubt, and spells of demoralizing blues. Though, knowing my mother's removedness, it's possible she wasn't anything too specific.

Far more than me, my mother is in touch—or at ease—with flows and overflow, particularly, and contends coolly, unusually so, with spats. For someone so angry about the state of things, fist up and ready to fight the fight, protesting and holding up banners or hanging them from her balcony, making calls on behalf of, hosting conference speakers at her home, showing up in solidarity, unionizing the teachers at her college, my mother does seem, on average, unbothered. There have been times when her disposition is equivalent to that of an email's auto-response away message: a calmly prompt, matter-of-fact no-show. She's *there*, but not exactly. My mother has proven that a person can be supportive yet remain unreachable, and how the combination has its virtues.

Despite my interest, there are moments from my parents' past that do not belong to me. The straw hat was, feasibly, nothing more than something silly you buy on vacation when you're young and in love, unburdened but married because marriage was made for the ill-prepared. And anyhow, strong winds blow away straw hats, or they collapse and splinter on the flight home. I've never seen a straw hat survive the state in which it was bought. Straws hats, in my experience, are whim-things. Unsubstantial.

There are nights when I go to bed a little foolish and pretend the world is a disco ball and that the stars are simply reflected dots. That none of this is too dire and how the impossibility of knowing everything is an advantage. Most children grow up and plan to, at some stage, sit with a parent, a pad of paper, a voice recorder, and listen. Most children, despite good intentions, never make it happen.

Perhaps we're waiting for our porch. We defer, defer, defer, and make excuses until we've won life's ultimate lottery: the porch. The kind that wraps around. There's something neutral about the conditions of its build: inside's privacy, but outside, it's an extension that stipulates the promise of delay. Imagine if our foreheads had porches jutting out from them? Maybe our brains would experience some reprieve.

On porches, conversation flows freely because silences, while weighty, aren't strained. The faint interruption of a neighbor's car pulling up the driveway or leaves rustling, or the benefits of a view in August, kink the air pressure that might exist between two people. A breeze jangles wind chimes and gently jolts us from ourselves. It's harder to speak selfishly on a porch. Even when it's hot, no one overheats. Picking a fight on a porch means you've missed the point entirely.

So, until then—until the porch or some semblance of it—we put off the pad of paper, the voice recorder. We are self-centered. We are out with friends, yet curious why. We are running late. Mentioning things in passing. Not picking up our phones. Lying on our stomachs. We are ambitious, only kind of. Obsessed to the point of—not boredom—but reprise. We are incapable of writing a letter of condolence. We are vulnerable when it suits us. Taking aim when wearied. Clumsily articulate when expressing intense feelings, like subtitles in a foreign film. We are in the midst of, or have just inched past, our *stretch*. We read a book that alters us but never talk to our parents about the books that change our fabric, so instead, the weather. The rain. The snow in April.

We are waking up to freckles dotting a person's back, and leveling that we might be in love—not with this person, but with freckles and downy morning light, because unfamiliar contours before nine a.m. have a way. With someone new, even freckles become spotless. They are a surface blurred and time deferred. Everything begins simply enough.

A friend who is in a play on Broadway recently sent me a picture of her dressing room. On her table are flowers, a patchwork of notes taped to her mirror, a tiny vile of dandelion fluff, a photograph of her aura—purples, some navy. For months now, we've been getting our auras photographed at this shop called Magic Jewelry on Centre Street that sells semiprecious stones and healing crystals. For twenty dollars—an extravagance I can't afford but can, so in that minute I spend it—we place our palms on metal sensors, have our photo taken with a Kirlian-type camera, and then sit and listen as an employee at Magic Jewelry—who sometimes speaks to us in the first-person plural—interprets the psychedelic colors of our aura. Reds and oranges mean one thing—that we've been working too hard, we've been told—and cooler colors signify that we're withdrawn and overthinking, daydreaming and negligent of more earthly forces. Habitually, the both of us are purple. Absent and worn-out. Entombed in thought. A distinguishing quality of the women I love, meaning, none of us are bothered by how infrequently we see one another. We have an arrangement that was never formally arranged. A consideration for turning down invitations. We are happy for the person who is indulging in her space, and how she might merely be spending the weekend unescorted by anything except her work, which could also mean: she is in no rush to complete much. She is tinkering. She is gathering all the materials necessary for repotting a plant but not doing it. She is turning off the lights and climbing into her head because that's usually the move.

In the years I've lived in New York, the women I've

made friends with seem not unfocused, and not absorbed by what's next or what happened days ago, but by what is marginally missing. As if they're trying to place a face when crossing a busy street. Women who seem satisfied when riding an escalator, who never fare well when they run into someone and are forced to reenter the world by speaking in banalities. The women I love reenter the world so poorly. Their elegance lies in how summarily they'll dodge its many attenuations, advancing alongside the world as if passing their fingers over the rails of a fence and cleverly selecting the right moment to hop over.

They are women who are loveliest when just a little bit haunted or mad as hell on a clear day. Who carefully believe in ghosts and kismet, and are mistrustful of shortcuts. Who laugh like villains. Wake up earliest when the sky is overcast. Who needn't say much for all to know, tonight, they won't be staying out long. Who dip their toes into the current, only to retreat and fantasize about the bowl of cereal they'd rather be scarfing down at home. Who, like my friend Jenny specifically, are hot. Who don't need anyone—including me right now—to depict why. Proximity to hotness can feel like a link to the universe. Your hot friend on a balmy summer night telling you about some good news in her life is—How do I put this without sounding absurd? It's barometric. It's love and someone you love's power growing, and it's watching the elements cater to a woman who exudes.

I won't go on more about the aura-photo-taking tradition my friend and I have, because the more one talks about
these extravagances, the more they invite questions that
cannot be answered. At any rate, some ceremonies exist so
long as they aren't solicited for profound meaning. They are
as is, hardly ceremony but what we repeat in order to make
sense of how disentangling personhood is. They are nothing
to effectuate. A lozenge that doesn't do much except taste
like honey. We get our auras taken in order to blueprint
the week or consider why we've been emotionally congested,
or, for kicks, plot some emotional solvency. We play with
life in order to play life, and often all a dark patch means is
a dark patch. Figurative, literal, neither, both. Take from it
what you will.

So one Monday afternoon, when my friend had a day
off, we ambled from midtown to Magic Jewelry, stopping
on the way for pea soup. A detail I cannot forget because
the pea soup was bright, bright green. Unnaturally so. It's
something we both noticed and continued to address with
each spoonful, because even the deepest friendships are
liable to remark on the color of soup. *Greeeeeen*, we said as
if it were slime. Delicious goo that seemed to establish our
day as one to remember, because from now on bright green
reminds me of the soup, which reminds me of my friend's
gold dress that she was wearing with black tights, and how
somewhere on Canal we dropped a letter for another friend
in a freshly painted mailbox. And how later, my friend

ordered apple-flavored sorbet, and me, tiramisu. And at night we ate a box of Thin Mints while she read my tarot, and then, as it happens, we talked about a boy who was once in a band.

Whenever my friend and I are together, our entire mode approximates switchbacks on a mountain railway. The zigzag required to climb. The *You were saying* that rounds our conversations and never anticipates close, like jelly legs from long walks, but, in this case, breathlessness from having talked so much and lost our train of thought as if losing it were a custom of recovery.

But back to her dressing table. On it, my friend's continued to collect objects like a curio cabinet of stuff that together becomes something. Her gallery. For the next five months, this parish of miscellany will provide my friend with the familiar. The way bedside tables become altars, and objects become testimonials, and candy bowls in dive restaurants: the perfect manifestation of *Until next time.* My friend's dressing table is what happens when the uncollected becomes a village of items, like a skyline formed from a row of shapes: the vile of dandelion fluff, a tube of lotion, a canister of Wet Ones. A yellow rose, now dried and dead, and somehow gilded as if when parched, the rose becomes royal.

There are the lucky few who zone out their windows and stare at brinks. The faraway intrigue of a forest—how it conspires—or the streaked lines of an ocean fringed by its horizon, or a city with more sky than scrapers, or even the informality of a backyard at dawn. But there are those—my friend and I—who can zone out, quite easily, to whatever's right in front of us, no matter how unspectacular. A poorly painted wall. Its cracks. The ceiling fan's chop. A woman on the C train pulling her ponytail through its tie, not once or twice, but six times. Six complete loops; her fingers closing into a claw each time. It'd been months since I'd been to a museum, but watching this woman mechanically tie her hair was softly enormous. Like the Apollo, the Lincoln Center at night, Film Forum's marquee—its lobby, its popcorn, perhaps not its seats. Like Rucker Park; like the screaming woman on East Seventy-seventh Street; like Dyker Heights at Christmas or the psychic with prime real estate and inexplicably zero clients ever; like the line outside Levain; like jumping out of the cab and walking instead; like speakers facing *out* apartment windows come summer and neighbors watering their plants, and sometimes watering their downstairs neighbors too, and like fire escapes in general; like an old eccentric in monochrome; the pinkness of Palazzo Chupi and Bill Cunningham blue; like a couple fighting for blocks, gesticulating crosstown and finally Cold Warring on the Hudson. Like Eastern Parkway on Labor Day; like Café Edison and Kim's before they were gone; like bodega cats and a bacon, egg, and cheese—a woman grooming on her subway commute is a New York institution.

I don't require much to feel far-removed; to impose my wanderings on what's close. Because of this, my friend and I have started calling ourselves nook people. Those of us who seek corners and bays in order to redeploy our hearts and not break the mood. Those of us who retreat in order to cubicle our flame. Who collect sea glass. Who value a deep pants pocket. Who are our own understudies and may as well have shadowboxes for brains.

We remember the soapy swoosh and high-pressure jets of car washes fondly. Of sitting in the backseat, near-worshipful of its cooped, walled-in chaos. We see a baby, burrito-wrapped in her blanket, and think, *Now, wouldn't that be nice?*

Nook people express appreciation in the moment by maintaining how much we will miss what is presently happening. Our priorities are spectacularly disordered. A nook person might spend the last few years of her twenties thinking she is dying. Convinced of it.

Nook people might be terrible at giving and receiving hugs despite often feeling—on the whole, at home and in public—as though we are holding on tight. Nook people sense slight tremors or the onset of a neck rash when faced with people at parties who yell-speak. A nook person catches sight of the quiet cranny at any gathering: the arm of a couch, a sill to perch on, the corner of a counter where the vegetable platter—only celery and ashy carrots are left—has been abandoned. A nook person finds the dog at the party;

drinks wine from a mug; sits on the floor and braids carpet tassels only to become self-conscious and unbraid them. From afar, even nearby actually, a nook person can seem like a real bore. The last person whom you want to meet. A fun-killer.

A nook person plays catch-up when someone's joke lands, embarrassed that her laugh isn't proportionate to just how funny she thought the joke actually was. *That was funny*, she'll say to compensate. Despite her many efforts, a nook person often suffers from a few-seconds lag.

Nook people know the words to a movie by heart but never say them out loud because anticipation is an asset. Because there's no interrupting Katharine Hepburn when she's interrupting herself: "Aren't the geraniums pretty, Professor?"

Nook people can overstate their love for a movie, having only watched it once. They are alert to how some spectacles become basically unbearable the second time. And, well, there are benefits to claiming something you've only experienced once as your favorite. It's useful to have many favorites. So many that you've depreciated the use of "favorite." Favorite. Favorite. Favorite. Who cares? At any rate, substantiating favorites is an absurd practice. The genius of the word is that it's more of an expression than a word.

Nook people have tricks. For instance, if I'm experiencing panic brought on by someone who leaves me fainthearted, I picture that person carrying with caution a just-filled ice tray back from the sink to the freezer. That image, on its own, can sometimes get me closer to where I'm meant to be. Just beyond the jam. Less impatient to compare myself. If I'm at an impasse and suddenly immovable, and unable to smile, I picture a plot of daffodils; how alien and dumb-eager they seem. Craning the way gooseneck lamps on desks—those too—look keen. I think about Little Flint introducing himself to Jane Goodall. Grown siblings being kind to each other. I wonder if penguins have knees.

Nook people are those of us who need solitude, but also the sound of someone puttering in the next room. Someone working on his project, down the hall and behind a door left ajar. We look away from our screen and hear him turning a page or readjusting his posture, and isn't it time for lunch? Resurfacing is nonpareil. And splitting a sandwich with someone you've said maybe two words to all morning is idyllic. A brief belief that life picks up after a few bites of toasted rye.

Though if I'm honest, the thought of splitting a sandwich suddenly makes me enormously sad. How long has it been since I've enjoyed the company of someone else enjoying his food? The way he'd toss chips in his mouth and savor the crunch, and then wipe his hands on his jeans, and smile—not at me specifically, but at this wonderfully unspectacular event: the sandwich, the chips, the crunch, our appetites.

Nook people need relief from distraction's overall insistence: the trap of everything else. Their ambition is not to be understood outright, but to return to an original peg. To share without betraying whatever mechanism individuates him or her. Perhaps that's what we call our disposition. How becoming is multipart, but mainly a pilgrimage inward. If you share too much of yourself, you risk growing into someone who has nothing unacknowledged. Those yet-to-access riches that I'd suspect are what tingle when a song's lyrics eject me into outer space; assure me I can love; can go about and be loved; can retreat and still *get*, as in both catch and understand, love. Those yet-to-access riches that I'd suspect too are what tingle when a building's architecture persuades me to notice other systems of proportion.

Or when an Annie Baker play sets in motion a story I'd like to write; an ex I'd like to call; a dinner party I'd like to have and invite Annie Baker to, and Sarah Polley, and Kareem Abdul-Jabbar, and Dolly Parton, and Shirin Neshat, my friend Judnick, and Eartha Kitt, were she still here, and one of my heroes, Polly Platt, were she still here too, and my stepfather, Mritiunjoy, because he's always good company, and my old super Sherlock, from my first apartment in Crown Heights, because he'd get along well with Mritiunjoy; with everyone really. It's that floating feeling—a light, invigorating sickness—that stems from seeing an Annie Baker play; that makes me want to make stuff instead of make sense, even if it's just a dinner party, or, quite the opposite, committing to a weeklong vow of silence.

Because nook people are turned on by and twig how terribly normal it is to drop out of life occasionally.

What a nook person wants is space, however small, to follow whatever image is driving her, instead of sensing like she might have to trade it in or share it before she's willing. Her awakening demands no stage but, rather room to store that second half of what she deems her double life: what's corrugated inside. Intuition's buildup.

Nook people find it trying to imagine themselves in real-life situations but long to climb into, for instance, a movie still. Into a pasture of wildflowers and tall grass and Merchant Ivory and Helena Bonham Carter's mane. Into *3 Women*'s desert pastels; those lenient yellows and corpse violets. Into Tom Hanks's Soho loft in *Big*. Every single frame of Maurice Pialat's *À nos amours*, but especially when Sandrine Bonnaire is dangling spaghetti into her mouth while a teenage couple makes out right next to her. Especially then.

Heat's floor-to-ceiling-windowed Malibu view, because a nook person forever seeks enclosed perpetuity. That Escher-like *Beetlejuice* house. Its patio. The discoverable mess of Elliott's closet in *E.T.* Or Céline's Paris apartment in *Before Sunset*. Where she's making tea and coyly dancing to Nina Simone, looking over her shoulder at Jesse to say, "Baby, you are gonna miss that plane."

Nook people are interested in what's backstage; are especially passionate about the small-scale bedlam of wimmelbooks; seek coats that cocoon; seek windows with shutters; a pattern that reveals itself over time; a vacation alone. Nook people can gently disagree while securing their spark. No. *No.* Spark is not substantive enough. Their approach. That radiant heat they typically keep stored inside because it functions as insulation.

Nook people love signing with a heavy pen; don't mind waiting in the car; love sitting on a stack of banquet chairs in an empty banquet hall, feet dangling; appreciate the surprising density of a beaded curtain; the weight of a pile of denim; gripping a large Fuji apple with both hands; the twine of Joni singing, *Oh, I could drink a case of you, darling* and wish they too could live in a box of paints.

Nook people fall asleep in their palms; are pacified by tucking their hands in the warm seam of two thighs; are rarely sure how they got good at anything; confront despair with a strong drink or by giving up for months, only writing first sentences or returning to a corrupted love; or converting their bed into a life raft, or wearing a thick cat-eye simply to walk to the store; or making innocent decisions like buying a shower radio to cure a bad day, or finding a friend who is folding her laundry and requesting that you sit on her floor while she pairs socks, or suggesting that you donate your bunch of brown bananas so that she might bake the bread.

Nook people confuse emotional truth with other varieties of truth. They are a composite of the last person who complimented them and the next person who might ignore them, and also whomever or whatever they consider themselves a child of.

As children, nook people so wished to be forgotten in department stores. Locked inside once the doors were closed. They were very good at hide-and-seek, perhaps even over-looking the game's reciprocal nature. Because when nook people find themselves lost briefly, they are stunned into a phenomenal sense of peace. Once, as a kid, I took a nap in the woods in the dead of winter because I couldn't find my way back to the farmhouse in upstate New York where my family was visiting friends. I'd walked in circles and confused my trail of footprints. Disoriented, all I could think to do was take a nap. I slept deeply, which is rare for me. As the sun began to set and as my parents began to worry, there I was snoozing soundly on a mound of snow, palisaded by a forest of bare trees and the holy, cease-fire quiet only nature can administer.

As adults, nook people cower under overhead lighting. They prefer when lamps yoke the floor rather than animate an entire room. They are habitual creatures who fear each time they're charmed by something, because what if it's the last time they are charmed by anything?

I keep a miniature pink flamingo on my desk at all times. It sits next to me when I type, like a charm that isn't a charm but a knickknack that proves I am not immune to superstition. If I lay it flat, the flamingo is smaller than my SHIFT key and just about the size of a date pit. The flamingo is rubbery and painted, and shaded as only mini things can be painted and shaded: so meticulously, so *verbatim*. It looks as if it's been zapped small from real life.

When I'm traveling, I tuck the flamingo into my purse. It sits next to a stuffed red heart that my friend—the one in the gold dress on pea soup day—gave to me. The heart fits into my palm—flat-round like a plush pebble—and was mailed to my friend with a box of other novelties, including the vile of dandelion fluff, I think. The heart, I learned, is from Build-A-Bear. I've never been to one of its stores or know much about it, but I've heard there is a tradition of placing the heart inside the bear while it's in the workshop. Maybe the employees blow on it? Or ask the customers to? Something like that. Maybe the children make a wish and rub the heart between their thumb and index finger the way adults test the touch of cashmere or gossip about someone's financial provenance. Either way, there is a ritual. How strange. How sort of gruesome and surgical. The most benign transplant, occurring in malls across America.

I think about my mother again. Young again. I wonder if she did in fact, like me, consider the fit of things: how the cherry liqueur gets inside the chocolate and if it's possible to sit on clouds. If cracking open scabs and peeling them off like bark on a tree was pleasing to her. If she dreamt about attics and the potential for troublemaking sloped ceilings provide. How everyone in an attic becomes a giant. How someone's head cautiously ducking under wood beams is, in some way, the universal symbol for explorer. Did they even have attics in Calcutta? Was the concept utterly foreign? Whenever I've asked my mother about what I deem rudimentary to child-wonder, like the mystery of attics, the word *dampness* repeats. Calcutta's dampness, that is. Like a relapsing obstacle for children born in tropical, wet-and-dry climates. *It was too damp for this, too damp for that*, she might say. Too damp for attics.

Or what about skylights. Did she have those? Know about those as a kid? How the sky seen through a skylight creates—at least in my mind—a more viable world. Isn't it cool how a skylight doesn't bring the blue inside, but instead influences a category of stupor? Everyone is reduced to aquarium eyes. There's no suspense in wondering what lies outside the frame, because skylights show bias but abet abandon. Bordered and mounted on a ceiling, a blue sky looks especially artificial, doesn't it? Like a portal elsewhere. Soothsaying.

I think about Build-A-Bear too. Would my mother have cared for one of those toys? Was she a child who hid things in other things? Was she curious about their make? The how? The *How?!* Had Build-A-Bear existed when I was a kid, would I have begged for one? Probably. The toys I wanted and never got as a child were one of many spites I held against my parents. It wasn't simply greed but superiority. The rank we pull as children of immigrants, believing our parents are, most days, confused or dead wrong. That they just don't know. That they'll get you a version of what you wanted; what's close will have to do. That they are uniquely assertive in the kitchen and don't pick up on cues, and smile reluctantly because smiling is the quickest way to appear as though you are aware. To mislead anyone doubting your ability. Especially your ungrateful children.

My sophomore year of college, my father had surgery to repair a valve tear in his heart. The edges were frayed. A vascular-ring Dacron connector graft was, I believe, used to stent the tear. The sutureless nature of it confuses me. While my father has explained how his valve was fixed, my mind is intent on dreaming up floating parts, like a valve that looks like a pool noodle or a ribbed dryer vent, and 3-D doodads rendered into 2-D graphics, and ducts and hoses, and bolts, and whenever I hear the word *frayed* I only think of jeans anyway.

Still, I do appreciate the consequence of the surgery. My father has since been semiretired from his job as an engineer and vice president for a company that, of all things, manufactures industrial valves. There is no irony to be lost, merely coincidence, and a broad reminder that, after all these years, I still have no idea what a valve does. How it works and for what purpose.

There are moments when I wonder if my ignorance stings my father. If my disinterest has offended him. There's a degree of apathy inherent to children and how they prefer to recognize, or insist on misunderstanding, their parents. There is too—how can I put this?—an unspoken expanse. The wilds that separate us. An acceptance that love has many versions and one of them is, plainly, the act of not knowing. An implicative bargain between parent and child that leans on time's mercy. Or maybe it's the *inaction* of not knowing. The lulls we favor in order for each member of a family to guard some sanity—to sit through traffic, clear the table without fuss, not ask who was on the other line.

Perhaps it's useful to classify this particular form of not knowing as different from the more existential crop of not knowing. This one involves more play. I choose to misread the workings of big, vital stuff like the heart, because, by and large, my preference to not know provides me with relief. How reinforcing it can be to create an untrammeled, let's call it "adjacent self" to my otherwise tightly wound, seeking self, who—much to the pain of anyone telling a story over dinner—is listening but requesting more detail. This other me tolerates occasional caprice; like imagining little men using a pulley-lever system to receive oxygen-rich blood into my heart. To my father's heart. Gluing together his valve. Grafting and sealing material that looks like a tube anemone.

My father's father, Amiya Kumar Bose, was a cardiologist. *Eminent in his field*, my father has reminded me ever since I was a kid. So much so that I now associate the characterization "eminent" as one specific to immigrant parents. One of their many *isms*—essential to their lexicon of pride. Of keeping the narrative strong and the achievements mantled. Of introducing their daughters as "My daughter *who* . . ." As though personhood is fixed to ability. As though parenthood is the practice of immodesty. Because awards and degrees, and recognition, and pioneering efforts in general, fade over time. They lose their shine, and sadly these feats so rarely translate. Masterpieces are paraphrased. They don't survive the journey or a grandchild's lopped retelling of them.

Growing up in Montreal, the folklore of family recipes was what my friends hyped. Secret ingredients for baked goods were somehow central. And guarded. But in my family, food was not the great family story. Food was the fabric. The basics. Dinner was elaborate but made quick. There was always rice.

My paternal grandmother, a statistician who'd go to work every day at the Writers' Building—shortened to Writers' by most—the red, Greco-Roman–designed secretariat building in Calcutta that housed the State Statistical Bureau Government of West Bengal, which later moved to the New Secretariat building on Strand Road, now that, *that* fact was repeated to me over and over. My grandmother Chameli was the director. She was in charge of an office of only men who called her "sir." A detail so ridged into my understanding of who she was that I've often imagined an office long and exaggerated, and practically surreal. An office in space. I've imagined men standing up from their desks as she arrived each morning; greeting her as she glided to her office in her sari. A woman gliding was—I'd devised—power incarnate.

Recently, my mother recounted a story to me about Chameli. One year, Chameli noted a statistical error in West

Bengal's rice farming figures; one that she deemed serious enough to change. The *dheki* is an agricultural tool used for threshing and separating the grain from the husk. It's composed of a wooden lever, a pedestal, and a pestle. Picture a rocket-shaped seesaw; the pestle like a walrus tooth pounding rice. In all village households, it was the Bengali peasant women whose job it was to husk the paddy into rice. While it was work, the work wasn't statistically counted as such. Those hours spent were negligible; ignored by virtue of being considered everyday household chores instead of hard labor. Chameli disagreed. She saw the gaffe as a severe misreading of numbers.

Here's the thing. By no means did my grandmother identify as a feminist. Quite the opposite actually. For her, fixing this error was merely a matter of valuing accuracy. For her, imprecision was totally substandard. When my mother told me this story, I thought about my grandmother gliding through her office, perhaps instilling acute fear in the men who reported to her. Scrutinizing their efforts. Suggesting they reexamine their data. The thought makes me grin.

I too was a bit scared of Thama. She could be mean. Often ailing but impassable. At no point would she back down; the sort of woman who is so obstinate that even the knot in her silk scarf looks stubborn, like a bulb unwilling to blossom. She was callous, brushing me aside by asking about my brother's day instead of mine. If I was wearing a new sweater, she'd ask me if my brother had gotten a new sweater too. There's a form of humiliation we learn to stomach young in order to receive attention. Mine was clarified by my relationship with my grandmother, whose fondness for my brother was openly warmer, even if her love was evenly spread.

Thama disciplined but seemed detached; a terrifying combination from a child's perspective. Her wood cane looked like it was up to something. A sidekick. A snake. Nowadays, I regret every second I spent with her where I didn't hold her hand or tell her I loved her, or showed her what I was reading or shared with her what I was thinking; who I was friends with; their names. I regret my teenage petulance. I regret the displeasure I wore in my posture. The unappealing stink that secretes from teenagers with a bad attitude who slope in their chairs and see only an old lady who's taking up a perfectly good Saturday in June. I was sad about the mushy, tasteless food my grandmother was forced to eat, but just as impatient that she eat it faster.

I regret how I wasn't gentler when combing her hair. Or how, more than once, I absently pushed her wheelchair into a door's frame. Or pushed her wheelchair too hastily back to her bedroom at the Grace Dart extended care center in Montreal East, where she lived the last years of her life. It's possible Thama would have enjoyed a more scenic route back to her bed—perhaps one that involved escaping the Grace Dart center entirely. Fleeing in her nightgown, somewhere less cold with a garden and trees, whose leaves reminded her of Calcutta sounds. A place too with an infinite supply of Pepperidge Farm hazelnut Pirouettes. She really enjoyed eating those rolled wafers, as if they were contraband.

I regret one afternoon in particular when Thama was asleep in her hospital room, snoring so quietly it sounded less like snoring and more like a person who'd lived many lives, simply breathing. That afternoon, when I was alone in her room, I noticed a vein protruding from her forehead. Like a cord of thick wale corduroy running down her temple. For no reason I can explain, other than some eagerness to touch, I pressed my finger against it. Thama kept sleeping. I touched it again and went further to push the purple blood that filled it, back up her vein, only to watch it rush forward as I let go. I did this a few times as if magic were involved. As if the tiny purple torrent were anything but blood. Kool-Aid. Dye. Beet juice. It was an odd impulse, certainly.

But even in hospitals, sunlight is beautiful. It animates the sterile and that feeling of sick. Brown cups look caramel and all that metal turns mauve, and Jell-O, well, Jell-O wins—it traps the sun. And suspended ceilings are hardly science fiction when the evening light thaws their grid. And the humiliation of loosely tied gowns and bare skin, and elastic waists, even those degradations fade some when the light pushes through blinds and discovers bare skin, not to shame but to warm. And on that day, the sun was beginning to dip and the purple blood was rushing back each time I pushed it up, and why was I doing this? Why wasn't I leaving her alone, to sleep her many lives? I regret touching her forehead like that, as if she weren't Thama but a new, random fascination. Her skin was jellyfish-transparent. Her fingers and knuckles were bent like gingerroots. She was fading. Shrinking. As if there were hardly any room inside of her to contain her memories. From here on out, Thama's memories would be forced out. They'd emit from her. They'd circle above her like cloud cover on a satellite map. You don't have to believe in ghosts to feel haunted by the draft of vanishing memories. I felt them that afternoon, escaping from her as the sun washed her hospital room with a little show. The sort of glory you only see when something else is being lost.

I was then, in that hospital room, dense about a lot and specifically about my grandmother. About her clout. It would be a long time until I would learn about the statistical error she corrected all those decades ago. A minor detail, but one that wows me. Quiets me proud. A facet of her character that reveals my grandmother's second ply. She was a scrupulous woman; compulsive about precision. She wasn't remedying those statistics in order to serve or fight for the rights of peasant women—outwardly, anyway—but because work was getting indexed improperly. It was how my Thama operated. What pressed her. No wonder my father insists on repeating stories about my grandmother. On remembering her like a zipper stuck on its slide. Chameli was a force. She had kick in her until the end, despite grumbling to me that God had forgotten about her.

My father's repetition, especially with regards to his family—especially when it comes to excellence—is fundamental to his speech pattern. As though his thoughts accrue but cannot prosper without checking in with what came before. Like his body domiciles the past. His tone is, time and again, commemorative—which I'll admit can grow tedious, though with parents it's good to keep one's cool. (Something I have yet to learn.) To heed one's frustration, because aren't we all disquieted by what we'll leave behind? What we won't. Aren't we all overrun by the blotting-out that is inevitable? How every year we claim that this year went by faster. What was realized? Did I connect? If I'm mostly—often only—the sum of what I've noticed; should I keep better track?

Did I discern between admiring and enjoyment? Did I try on a dress? Even once? Did I disturb some peace? Experience some peace? Was I strong physically? How many times did I say yes when I should have said no? Can someone, please—anyone—devise a "no" that clarifies how *no* serves many reactions? How it can deliver beyond its blunt, single unit of speech? A "no," for example, with less glare. A shallower, vaporous "no." A "no" that riffs off "nope" but is more nimble.

Did I drink less? Sleep more? Eat more? Was I a body? And did the boundaries of my thighs and the span of my arms inform my flight, or were they limbs only? Swinging, stretched, crossed. Folded around me and furthering that feeling of deadweight when I wake up in the morning and think, *Again?* When I wonder if it's possible to deplane from this week; from this period in life.

Did I listen to *Tidal* in its entirety instead of "Shadow-boxer" on repeat? *Illmatic* in its entirety? *The Miseducation* without skipping over Lauryn's interludes? Did I recover from the minor tragedy of gifting someone I love earrings she will never wear? Did I finally admit defeat and stop photographing sunsets?

Did I properly mourn my mother's maple tree? She loved that century-old tree. It was, in a word, providing. When the city cut it down in February because of a vertical split they deemed dangerous, she sent me an email with the subject line: "our tree—RIP." Attached was a picture from the scene outside her living room window. Our snowy front lawn powdered with sawdust and two city workers in neon orange, severing fallen branches into smaller logs. The tree's stump looked irrelevant. And even though I couldn't hear the violent, hacking buzz of their saws, I could. A vibration that tapers and starts over, tapers and starts over, like a terribly fatiguing and stubborn goodbye. This will be my mother's first summer without her maple. But summer is not intended for withouts. So what now? As with all endings, nothing suits. In July we'll play Scrabble on the balcony; unprotected, in view. A sudden rainstorm will no longer feel abundant. The green is gone. That magically indistinct quality of dancing leaves and their shadows, and how it's impossible to tell where branches begin, end, and reach, unless a squirrel darts or a breeze gets rowdy. Will we miss the tree or move on and grow accustomed, and tolerate this new opening as an understanding?

What new habits did I develop to cut myself off from the world? When will I learn that those habits are, it's possible, delimiting me from innocuous connections. Someone to sit next to on a couch too small, flipping the pages of a book too big, where the pages graze my sweater's stomach, and I can't pin why, but the whole small-big ratio of pages grazing my sweater creates an impression of secrecy.

Someone to wish well before his trip to Tokyo; to call when I can't sleep. To share a bowl of blanched almonds with, sitting on stools—small again too—that force my knees to bend at right angles, which feels somehow athletic. Which is, by nature, suggestive.

Someone to provoke me; to watch Game 7 with; to accompany to a gallery where I don't care for the art, but oh, how I love being in the vicinity of someone I confide in daily, whose posture is distinguishable, even under the lumpy mass of her winter coat, her scarf, the infantilizing fit of her boots. When will I learn? Nobody knows you're thinking of him, of her, of our walk along the Thames, eight years ago I think it was, after seeing Peter Doig's white canoe at the Tate, unless you call or write and say so.

This year, was I competent? Did I referee my whims or

elaborate on them? Did I express gratitude? Feel the potency of night? Accept an offer to stay over without reciting the many excuses I use to screen my doubts?

How quickly did I quit my diary? How many ballet documentaries did I watch? Re-watch? What is it about ballet documentaries?

Why, come spring, do I get restless and talk *at* the people I hold nearest, dearest, instead of talking *to* them? Did I love extravagantly? Kick the ground, rip the lining, get loud with bourbon, rest my head on someone's lap and fall asleep? Did I paint? Or use pencil crayons to shade the shy carriage of a pear? Did I enjoy the short-term taste of believing an idea I had arrived at was rare?

Or maybe it's beneficial to abandon abstractions about how it'll all come into being and subsist, alternatively, on touch, smell, Doreen's laugh, Satyajit Ray, a poem's scald, my stepmother Lisa's compassion—her Irish scones too. Miniature awakenings that, with any luck, open one up to love or let go of one's servitude to external validation. Miniature awakenings that keep me vulnerable to moonbeams and allow feelings to pathfind. To return to an original springboard and jump off again. And then again. Remember the feel of wet cement under your feet at the pool? Of shivering in line and climbing the ladder. The *splash!* How ordinary it became to splash. And then climbing back out, and shivering and dripping. The cool redundancy of doing the same thing over and over because summer's inculpability meant it was possible to become your own encore.

When my father repeats himself, he is not just reminding me of his parents' lives; my father is coerced by the rubbing-out that comes with remove. How it can rarify a family's history. Nobody was going to tell your story unless you told it yourself. And nobody was going to remember it unless you repeated it enough for your story and for your memories to develop their own rhythm.

Because memory is lying in wait, and then, out of nowhere, something blisters. Builds. Sails. Memory is especially choral if the story recalls a childhood pet. Like Duane. My father's spitz, named after Duane Allman, who one day in Calcutta raced off the balcony and fell three stories, landing on a herd of sheep crossing the street. Duane survived his fall, and I've heard that story about the sheep-shaped trampoline again and again, and I've often asked it be retold despite knowing it by heart. My parents' histories, those quiet storms and units of time—the flying spitz, the mischief at St. Xavier's—sound better when they tell it, because there will be a time when they are no longer here to tell it.

History is not indelible. History hardly exists. History is a pool of questions that begin with "Whatever happened to?" History is not—on its own—staunch. History is not the number of suitcases you moved with, the plants you carried with you, the people you left behind. History is an obligation that ages you. It trips you up. It skulks and grovels, particularly for those trying hard to move on. History is the daughter repeating to her friends that you moved with two suitcases full of LPs, or that you fell in love and knocked on his door and announced you were moving in—with your plants, of course. With not much else.

Time's erasing duplicity, the lost elements, an uncle in a photo whom we only know by his nickname or an earthquake where the walls shook for minutes and Elvis, my cousin's tabby, hid between my legs, and all these things, like a daughter who might not grasp or care for certain connotations, who for years assumed the word *eminent* was boastful instead of accurate, these are the reasons we repeat.

Born on Christmas Day in the year 1900, my grandfather died a month short of his seventy-fifth birthday, three or more months into Indira Gandhi's declared Emergency. That my father's father would never know his son had two children is a sorrow that doesn't loom, so much as, sporadically, I get the sense, my father is hit with the hypothetical: *Imagine he could have met you.* There's an understanding that my grandfather would have liked me. Loved me, sure. But liking is altogether different. It's gentle. Almost chewy. Liking someone is taffy.

The moment one hears that sentiment expressed—that someone who has passed would have enjoyed you—one begins to carry it. I heard it young, and I became, in little ways, curious about what in me he might have found interesting. He would have, I'm convinced, asked me about my friends. Pronounced their names fondly. One of my top five favorite sounds: when my family enunciates my friends' names with an odd emphasis on certain syllables. Rachel became Raaaaay-chel. Collier is suddenly French, like the word for necklace. My friends India and Echo have been tagged together and confused, and I rarely insist on correcting the mix-up because how are parents expected to keep up? They shouldn't have to. Elana is pronounced "Uh-La-nuh," which seems correct enough, though there's a trace of casual melody in my parents' accents, especially my mother's. So even "Elana" sounds like the name of a song by a seventies folk band my mother might have listened to on tape.

Over the years my mother has mentioned in passing how she thinks my father should have, like his father, been a doctor. He is, it's true, the first person in my family anyone calls when there are questions about a cough, a lump, an ongoing pain. He knows what to do, how to heal. Who to call. The next logical step. He accompanies his aging friends to physiotherapy and, at night, to the emergency. He sits and waits. He fills prescriptions. Buys them new pants when, in sickness, they've lost weight. And new ones when they've gained it back, to mark the occasion. He cares for those not lucky enough to have grown children. He gives rides. Buys and delivers bags of basmati rice.

When there was a tear in my father's valve, I wondered if he missed his father; if he spoke to him in his head and went forth with a small amount of heritable wisdom.

If in those days leading up to his surgery he was, once again, a son.

The day of his surgery, I sat in my college's dining hall clutching my phone, waiting for the call from my stepmother where she'd say, choked-up but relieved, that everything went well. I was with two friends who were talking about another friend, and I remember thinking how noisy friends can be. How they are, at times, battery-powered clamor and emotionally expensive, and briefly I wondered, *Why have friends?* Why sit through their noise when what I needed was an impossible silence. There's no such thing as the silence one needs. It doesn't exist because need is loud. So I sat and listened to my friends and clutched my phone, and then, without noticing it, a tear slid down my cheek. My nerves had burst but my face was numb. My friend reached her hand across the table and touched my arm, and what's more, she didn't ask why I was crying. She barely made eye contact. We were each other's tolerable silence. Energy between two people can feel the opposite of energy. The most muted, beloved bailout.

In the late John Gregory Dunne's book *Monster*, in which the critic and novelist recounts his experiences as a screenwriter in Hollywood, cowriting scripts with Joan Didion, his wife, many sections are devoted to Dunne's weakening heart, and the cost—both financial and physical—that powered and metered his work. In the interest of covering the price of doctors' visits, tests, and hospital bills following his first collapse, in 1988, while speed walking in Central Park, Dunne needed to remain a member of the WGA in order to benefit from the union's health insurance plan. Consequently, Didion and Dunne wrote movies: *The Panic in Needle Park* (1971), an adaptation of Didion's *Play It as It Lays* (1972), *A Star Is Born* (1976), an adaptation of Dunne's Black Dahlia murder case–inspired *True Confessions* (1981), and *Up Close and Personal* (1996), of which the eight-year, twenty-seven-draft saga is detailed in *Monster*. "We've written twenty-three books between us," he told *The Paris Review* in 1996. "And movies financed nineteen out of the twenty-three."

In 1991, Dunne underwent aortic valve replacement surgery at Columbia-Presbyterian and recovered in the hospital's McKeen Pavilion. Throughout *Monster*, Dunne avoids indulging in every writer's more obvious belligerence; our fixation and phobia with End. How to ward it off in our work and still conclude with presence, hope. A hatch. Even when Dunne describes first fainting that crisp February morning in Central Park, the episode seems cursory. "I was stretched out in the middle of the road rising behind the Metropolitan Museum," he writes, describing regaining consciousness seconds after his collapse. "A stream of joggers detouring past without looking or stopping, as if I were a piece of roadkill." The image would be gruesome if it weren't for the Met. For the joggers. For the whole uptown mise-en-scène. Or perhaps it's gruesome because of it. Life could end—conk!—at any moment, and uptown joggers might treat you like New York roadkill, and hours from now, the Met will be mobbed with tourists wearing sensible walking shoes. And you've been swatted down, and tomorrow the joggers will return, running faster, having improved on their times. And the tourists—still in town, wearing their sensible shoes—will be riding the ferry to Ellis Island or eating pastrami at Katz's.

Though, in a rare moment of self-reflection, Dunne describes the replacement valve's clicking sound and how it signified "reassuring proof [he] was still alive." This newer, louder heartbeat was a reminder of his impermanence and how in illness, what's been assumed can no longer be assumed. We develop a habit of converting the everyday into souvenir. Of holding off what's meaningless. That, or we veer off script. Illness compels us to ad-lib. As Katharine Hepburn once suggested—again Hepburn because she's never far from my mind—"Wouldn't it be great if people could get to live suddenly as often as they die suddenly?" To live without delay. To *come to* just as tersely as death *comes for*. I'd like to think Hepburn—who I'm now picturing in a photo I've seen of her riding a skateboard wearing a white pantsuit—I'd like to imagine she meant, despite all of its concerns, that life should be lived unusually.

The clicking from Dunne's plastic valve, which replaced his calcified one, also resonated with his daughter, Quintana. The *click, click, click* entertained her. She began calling her father the Tin Man. When I first read *Monster*, Quintana's nickname for Dunne reminded me of that scene near the end of the movie where the Wizard tells the Tin Man, "As for you, my galvanized friend, you want a heart. You don't know how lucky you are not to have one," he warns. "Hearts will never be practical until they can be made unbreakable." Regardless, the Tin Man still desires one. He's tired of sounding like an empty kettle. Of never *registering emotion*, he sings at the movie's start. The Tin Man wants all of it. For his soul to light up. To feel the hot swell of *jealousy*, *devotion*, he continues. To *really feel the part*.

Those four words, as plain as they are, toll. An unassuming way of saying he's ready to be human. Or possibly, some impersonation of it. The role of humanhood as he's imagined it.

But to consider his song as such, tilts the sentiment. To *really feel the part*, the Tin Man needs his prop: a heart. It's fundamental to the costume. Perhaps I'm overthinking it and the Tin Man has it all figured out. The *lub-dub* sound is what's keeping record after all. Evidence of a narrative build. Maintenance despite life's lows; its howling moods and those days when you find yourself in bed before dinner with the windows open, disaffected by the sounds trickling in. How mobile those sounds are: a neighbor riffling through a cutlery drawer; sandaled feet on dusty pavement; a fire engine's ungainly siren.

Even when life presents one disincentive after the next—"I'm fine," she'll say. "It'll be okay," she insists unconvincingly. Even when hopes aren't met or the comedown from an emotional night cedes to birds chirping before five a.m.—which, honestly, is too early for birds to chirp—even then, despite the guilt you feel from greeting morning having not yet slept, the heart stays lub-dubbing. Even when love is unreturned; when I've been hurt but refuse to get furious—would I even know how?

Even when someone forces you to articulate what you find intolerably hard to articulate, the heart is at work. On board, howbeit. In this way, the heart seems inhuman. Or actually, superhuman. It doesn't acquiesce. It's motored. It's motiveless.

In her 2004 book, *Don't Let Me Be Lonely: An American Lyric*, Claudia Rankine considers Mr. Tools, who, in July 2001, was the world's first recipient of a self-contained artificial heart. "His was a private and perhaps lonely singularity," notes Rankine. "No one else could say, I know how you feel." Mr. Tools didn't have a heartbeat but a whirr. "It was not the same whirr of a siren, but rather the fast repetitive whirr of a machine whose insistent motion might eventually seem like silence," she writes. "The weight on his heart was his heart." Mr. Tools survived 151 days with his artificial heart, dying at the age of fifty-nine in Louisville, Kentucky, from complications unrelated to the heart device.

Neither Dunne's clicking valve nor Mr. Tools's heart-whirring seems like particularly strong sounds. More like test sounds. In Dunne's case: metallic. Or as Rankine wrote of Mr. Tools: "If you are not Mr. Tools, detectable only with a stethoscope." They are sounds *in place of*. Proof not of life but of proof. Another symbol for "heart," like the plush Build-A-Bear heart, like our fingers butting up against one another and held in front of the left side of our chest. Just yesterday my phone autocorrected "heart" to "hearse." Sometimes when I send emails from my phone while riding the subway underground, the blue sending bar that slowly crosses the bottom of my screen looks like a heart monitor flatlining. Doesn't the red "low battery" symbol on our iPhones glow like E.T.'s heart?

Ten years ago I was in Mumbai with a friend I've since fallen out with. We were visiting another friend whom, as time has passed, I've also lost touch with. The three of us were there for New Year's, and my friend and I—the one I fell out with—were traveling back to Kolkata by train once the trip was over, and then back to New York shortly after. At first, the idea of Mumbai was exciting. Visiting friends in foreign cities usually is. *Isn't this crazy?!* we'll say upon reuniting. *Completely wild*, we'll nod. The extreme familiar—a close friendship—reoriented by the extreme unfamiliar is usually a formula for fun. All the qualities of a new experience in the company of someone who lessens the overstimulation sometimes brought on by new experiences. This is why we laud people who make good travel companions. We value that mix of curiosity, of limiting impatience for the trip's duration, of being responsive, even-tempered, but also willing to skip the museums and spend whatever money you have left on day drinks and aimless walking.

But in Mumbai, I remember drinking too much vodka and feeling restless. Like I couldn't figure out why I was there. Like I was meant to be having fun—so much of it—that as a reaction, my anticipation had soured. I was in possession of all this freedom, traveling with a friend, visiting another friend, and yet, I felt hollow. Looking out an apartment window, standing on a balcony, returning to my book, barely reading, thinking of perhaps sightseeing, not knowing where to start. Waking up early and badly wishing for the chatter only a family can provide. That nothing-talk that grows lively for no reason. Ten years ago was too young to know friends who chatted in the morning. It still might be.

But one morning I was given a task. My mother called and asked, since I was the only immediate family from Canada in Mumbai at the time, if I'd visit my cousin's husband's mother who was recovering in the hospital. She had undergone heart surgery. I was thrilled. Something to do. A destination. I could leave my friends, the vodka, the lazing around, and arrive somewhere. I got dressed, decided to wear a pair of dangly earrings, and grabbed a shawl my mother had loaned me for the trip.

Downstairs, my friend waved over an auto-rickshaw and in Hindi instructed the driver where to go. I understood none of what he said, but smiled, climbed in, and stared at the map I'd drawn that now looked like nothing at all. A few lines, a turn I'd emphasized by going over it a few times with my pen, some more lines, a big loop. The scribble had made more sense moments ago, but now that I was in the auto-rickshaw, among life as it zipped past me—two wedding processions; daylight waning; immeasurable traffic—I hoped the driver knew where he was going.

An hour went by. We'd stopped twice for directions. I showed anyone willing to help, my map—the lines, the turn, the more lines, the big loop. I said "Heart Hospital" over and over. *Heart Hospital!* Of course that wasn't the name of the hospital. It was called the Asian Heart Institute. But somewhere along the ride, the rickshaw driver started saying heart hospital and so I started saying heart hospital. Whenever someone giving directions would nod, I would nod. He nods. I nod. And so on. But shared nodding in a country where you don't speak the language is, I learned, the same as saying, *Yes, yes, yes.* But what were we agreeing on? Was I simply trying to keep the mood light and not look too confused? "HEART HOSPITAL," I enunciated. The more I pronounced the words, the more the words lost all of their meaning. Say anything too much, and soon language becomes pummeled nothing. Totally estranging, inadequate, and without substitute. Your tongue may as well be numb.

By the time it got dark, we had driven on all kinds of roads. The driver's handlebar steering revved loudly as if accepting a new challenge each time we curved around and inched between cars. Oddly enough, I never grew anxious. A deep calm nestled inside of me like my nerves were newly insulated. Like when a dog chooses my lap to curl up on. Like when a sweater is too long in the arms. Like when nobody is speaking and nobody feels pressed to.

Anything could be just outside this doorless, trembling auto-rickshaw. The unreal, even, like raging water, bare desert for miles—and it wouldn't matter. I was disoriented yet deaf to concern because I only experience the candied tang of what's imminent—the possibility of drawing near—when I am truly lost. When hope is a weak vital sign. A low ticking. A glowbug.

Maybe I would never arrive at the heart hospital. Maybe it didn't exist. Maybe I was lost in Mumbai. The trip had felt like nothing up until now. As far as I was concerned, failing to find something was greater than having nothing to look for. So I let go. I leaned back against my vinyl seat. I closed my eyes. I felt the road's bumps—a replenishing, gentle shock each time. I felt the abrupt, crass smoothness of highway. I felt the night's breeze, my own breathing, and sounds approaching, and horns passing. I heard unspecified purring like a score of whispered secrets, sped up and looping, and just a bit sinister. More so than daytime noises, nighttime noises wreathe.

With my eyes closed, I felt like I was flying. Arbitrary images popped into my mind as if what screens inside my eyelids is half haunted and clipped of story. Those tousled and nearly unaccounted-for impressions. Those observations that go nowhere yet enrich my memory—incongruous, random, and without incident, like found footage. Like the sheared memory of Christmases; the topography of someone I love's palm; roof tar sticking to my shoe; a skinny cat's rib cage; the rubbery satisfaction of yanking a single blade of grass from its root; the sound of someone setting a table for lunch in the garden and those intervals of silence where she looks up at the sky to weigh the threat of dark clouds and how fast they're moving, and in looking up, she wickedly obscures who has more power—the incoming storm or the woman bargaining with it by placing cloth napkins as winds pick up.

Even more indiscriminate thoughts collage. Like my irrational fears: dryer lint, the void that hollows a spiral staircase, or the several ways I feel illegitimate whenever I allow myself some latitude. Or feeling somehow fidgety when there's unexpected legroom on a plane; the ugly manner in which my face warps when big tears are about to overwhelm me, and how repressing them means deforming my cheeks and chin and forehead as though a leech is swimming frantic beneath my skin. Or the power that composes me when I walk down the aisle of a moving train. Or the coppery taste of blood; the slippery touch of cherry seeds; signing my name on condensation; the novelty of a round window; how little I know about birds. How the string section of an orchestra appears hypnotized, far more than the brass and woodwind; how at the grocery store, spotting the bottom hem of a woman's nightgown under her raincoat feels classified. Or how awkward it is to be in the company of a friend who's expressed to me that I've been inconsiderate and self-absorbed, and how attempting to mend my pattern is graceless, pinching, and worse, feels false. How being hard on myself is, oddly, a lazy system for letting myself off the hook. How sometimes I imagine hubcaps spinning off the wheels of cars and slicing me in two. How a coral shirt I rarely wear compels my friends to argue whether the shirt is *more salmon* than coral, and even if the difference is slight, sometimes it's nice to hear voices I admire boom emphatically over dumb, trifling things.

The memory of peering into my cousin Samantha's bedroom surfaces. I was small, no older than ten, and I spotted a biography of Marilyn Monroe tossed beside a pair of black Dr. Martens boots, and Samantha caught me looking and slammed the door, and instantly Marilyn Monroe and Dr. Martens were the most forbidden. Or my mother's crooked teeth. Fanged and disobedient. Crowding her mouth like concertgoers front row, pushed up against the stage. They are my favorite set of teeth because when my mother smiles her teeth resist any notion that happiness is an upshot of perfection. Her smile is chaotic. Teeming, toppling, and lovely.

"Madam . . . madam."

I'd closed my eyes just long enough to have dozed off.

"Madam," the driver said again. "Museum."

I slowly came to and felt my mascara unstick between my lashes.

"Museum, madam."

"Museum?" I asked.

"Heart museum."

Oh no, I thought. He'd brought me to a museum in the middle of the night. I looked out and saw nothing.

The driver pointed up ahead. "Heart museum."

This couldn't be right. "No, no." I shook my head. "Hospital. *Heart hospital.*"

"Heart museum," he repeated.

A museum? At night? I lifted my chin, suggesting we should drive up the road some more.

The driver was now smiling as we inched closer. As the rickshaw pulled up to the front, I peered out and saw what looked like a very fancy hospital. That's how I remember it at least.

"Heart museum, madam," he said once more.

I nodded, thanked and paid the driver, and walked toward the entrance. It had become chilly and I was grateful to have brought the shawl with me. Quietly moved by the rickshaw driver's construal of this large, looming building, I climbed the stairs. Even though this was a hospital and in visiting family I was only doing my daughterly duty, his characterization of "Heart Museum" recuperated in me what I was so longing for: a sense of arrival. The words "Heart Museum," like a figurative place; a vault where memories shimmer, fall dark, are cut loose, and unexpectedly flare up when you most need them to. The words "Heart Museum," like an experiment; twitchy, sad, parceled, soulful, like Arthur Russell. The words "Heart Museum": a meaning archive; a parent's medicine cabinet with expired sunscreen and old Band-Aids; the contents of a care package; a hideout for mind and spirit; mausoleum-*like*. The words "Heart Museum," like the essence of a word from another language for which English has no word. Because is there anything better, more truthful and sublime than what cannot be communicated? The marvelous, hard-to-spell-out convenience of what's indefinite.

2

Part of a Greater Pattern

THE dead squirrel was, without a doubt, going to make me very late for school. *Stupid squirrel*, I thought while brushing my teeth, staring at its fig-shaped body floating facedown in our swimming pool. As a kid I was—in my way—quick to wind up. To set off. Something primitive and stormy would kindle in my chest, and I would become possessed by shivers of short temper; an eleven-year-old who hated being late, whose grumbling irascibility my mother never claimed. "You didn't get that from *me*," she'd stress. Which was, in her way, a manner of getting wound up at my father.

Staring at the dead squirrel's body from my bedroom, which overlooked our backyard, I imagined our pool festering with rabies. Miasmic ripples forming a paisley pattern around its furry corpse. "Stupid squirrel," I might have even said out loud.

Having shared a room with my brother until I was

eight, this bedroom all to myself was my first encounter with privacy. While its green shag carpet was hideous, it encouraged—as ugly, funny, and unfair things do—my incurable taste for the make-believe. Stories flickered as I'd lie down, press my cheek against its itchy surface, rake my fingers through the carpet's deep pile, thumbing its loops and sharpening, with one eye open and one eye closed, my focus. Entire worlds existed in that green shag carpet, like I devised entire worlds in the mazelike depths of movie cornfields, for instance, or in secret gardens, in pictures of missing children whose lives I guiltily romanticized, or behind ominously big doors where rich people lived on the Boulevard near Montreal's Mount Royal, in mansions so tall they muddled my spatial awareness and seemed to taper on top like spires.

Because it was our family's first house with two floors and a basement, it was also my first backyard. My first rhododendron, which blossomed fat and white, blushing pink right before the petals molted. My first lilac bush too. The flowers' sweet, heady smell would last on my fingers long after I'd cut the stems and carried around the cone-shaped whorls, sometimes doing laps of our block, pretending the lilacs had been given to me by some imaginary admirer. So dreamlike was this admirer that true-to-life details of who he might be weren't of consequence. He was unrealized. A feeling. Many feelings, actually. A shimmering buildup of Boy. The sort of montage-person we conjure as kids, scraped from that corner in our imagination devoted to believing a character on TV—in my case, Gus Pike from *Road to Avonlea*—and the guy at the video store were maybe the same person.

The backyard was also my first acquaintance with a wood-paneled fence. Well actually my first acquaintance with those slits between the panels—my aperture—where I could spy our neighbors doing boring things like water the grass or race inside to grab a ringing telephone. No matter how dull whatever I observed was, a fairly hectic and illicit surge would course through me. The devotional quality of someone going about his or her day, of having to stand on her tiptoes to secure the corner of a bleach-stained towel on her clothesline or pace and pause, pace and pause, while talking on his cordless phone, was an intimacy I'd never deemed intimate until it belonged to a stranger who had no idea I was bearing witness. The thrill of a quick look provided me with pure, almost hysterical voltage.

The inground pool came with the house and was, as my father had predicted, his burden for us to enjoy. Our first summer there, the pool company who drained and refilled it with a hose fished out two or three bras they'd found at the bottom of the deep end. It was rumored the bras belonged to our neighbor's teenage daughters, who would go skinny-dipping once the previous owner—an older woman named Madame Dorée, whom I've resolved must have looked like Anne Bancroft with less sting or Maria Callas with less agony—was fast asleep. The found bras, which I never saw but pictured elementally, presuming they were neon pink or lacy and black, like filigree culled from our pool's gross winter grime, were the height of teenage girl trouble. Right in our backyard! The proximity both scandalized and, of course, intrigued me.

Older girls, like babysitters or a friend's sister in high school, were pedestaled beings with perfect jean jackets. They were white girls mostly. Close-talkers with side-swept bangs who never appeared too wowed by anything, because they had yet to and might never encounter what it means to be denied. I coveted their casual nature, believing their incuriosity was a sign of self-possession; of not harboring some secret longing to be seen. Seen alone, not in comparison or as other, or through the bewildering construction of compliments that seemed to only further other.

What I noticed first was their hands. These older girls had chipped nail polish like shrinking enamel continents on each finger, in colors like baby blue or black. They wore big sweaters, which they'd pull over their hands and rip open holes like harnesses for their thumbs. On those thick digits I'd spot their silver thumb rings that seemed fastened on the way flange nuts thread onto screws.

Even their bad skin conveyed a type of beauty that desperately drew me in because it wasn't beauty alone. It was notional. What I perceived as built-in unhindered-*ness*. Like ripping and ruining one's clothes at one's pleasure. Drawing with ballpoint pen on the rubber sidewall of one's Converse—a truly satisfying motion, actually. It was things done *just because*. It was disinterest. Inconceivable amounts of it. How exquisite I thought it would be to not care.

These older girls were impulsive. They dyed their hair on a Monday night. They threw parties when parents were home. As I remember, a good amount of these white girls wanted to become marine biologists. Their copies of Sarah McLachlan CDs or Janet Jackson's *The Velvet Rope* were well loved and scratched, skipping in unison to the grinding *bump bump bump* on "I Get Lonely."

These older girls' mannerisms were big and loud, and slumped too, as though they'd portioned a limited quantity of enthusiasm per week. They could exert influence—I'll never know how—by merely arriving to school with wet hair that would air-dry by second period. In comparison, these older white girls made the rest of us appear like we were waiting in perpetuity. For what? It didn't matter. The rest of us were girls-postponed.

In groups, their attention was coaxed elsewhere. Fatigued by whatever buzz was proximate, they observed in its place someone in the periphery, like that boy on his skateboard whose cheeks would get flush on autumn days—blotchy like deli meat. If you ever passed him in the hall, he smelled like an unwashed fitted sheet. At lunch, he vaulted off and grinded on curbs, rarely speaking to anyone and wearing a seemingly empty knapsack that looked like a deflated pool toy strapped to his back. While nobody knew much about him, there was an older girl who was likely intent on holding his hand and meeting his dog—now old and slow, but who still followed him from the pantry to the fridge to his basement bedroom because this dog and this boy had been buddies for years. This older girl was hoping to sit on the edge of this boy's unmade bed, expecting tenderness only to receive none, and gaze at the reproach of his dresser's vista: loose change, the glint of empty gum packets, a picture of him from camp with a girl from Ottawa she didn't recognize, a stereo, CDs, weed crumbs, the bald head of his deodorant stick missing its lid. She'd spy his copy of *1984* and desperately wish they were in the same English class.

These older girls created landmarks out of picnic tables. Or wherever they'd congregate at recess to smoke. Adjacent places. Adjacent to where they were meant to be standing. Like just beyond the bus stop. Like in the parking lot next to the pizza place. Under an awning. Under an overpass. Behind the rink. It wasn't solely that everywhere they went people followed, but that these older girls knew to show up mid-throng. When there would be cigarettes to bum, a boy's sweatshirt to borrow on a windy day, someone else's fries to stave off eating at all. Someone else's Cherry Coke. These older girls would steal one sip because there was always, somehow, a straw bent in their direction. They had a knack for arriving just in time to: *know all the words*. When the song was well into its chorus or nearing Left Eye's verse.

These older girls seemed satisfied by suggesting someone scoot over. They'd often plop themselves on a lap, or lean their weight into another white girl's body with the kind of collapse that courts attention. These older girls' comfort with one another was physical, though I'd mistaken it all those years ago as psychic. They knew nothing, or so it seemed, about the prickling and pining so innate to me; about deeply honed unease. These older white girls petted each other.

They'd roost, and still do, in the bedroom where all the coats are piled during parties, lounging and talking with impish flair because beer spumes festive around sequins. Because wearing heels indoors on wood floors sounds like the holidays. Because secrets stumble out like small talk when you are beautiful and everyone is listening. Because catching your reflection in a host's full-length mirror is a rare come-on. And because participating, for these older girls, meant, and maybe still means, reorienting a party's habitat—means loafing on a bed of coats.

I was, back then, a decade or so away from clocking my brownness, from taking notice of its veiled prominence in my life. I wasn't so much blind to it, but uninvolved in it. Emotionless about it. I was a brown daughter too inclined by whiteness to appreciate that being a daughter extends beyond the home. That it's a furtherance. That my parents were handsome, strong, willing. Adaptable. Selfless. Brilliant. Beautiful. I was too busy troubling myself with what I thought was pretty.

So I cloistered my brownness. I wasn't yet ready to scrutinize my weird, even toxic, relationship to the exclusionary appeal of these older white girls. To their ubiquity. To their immunity. I was coaxed by my stewed and crummy and, invisible to me, feeling of inferiority. In turn, I praised these girls for the faintest reasons. I was convinced they'd never be caught sucking in their stomachs. That even the tiny grooves of their anatomy could transmit persona: a dimple or belly button shaped like a comma. Meaning: *She always had more to say.*

I held that their overall manner was epitomized by how impossibly cool they looked when doing plain things. Like pulling something, anything—it didn't matter what—from their back pockets, or casually hoisting their butts onto a kitchen counter midconversation. Their thighs didn't seem to pancake like mine when I'd sit down; their knees weren't shapeless either. I call mine potato knees. Inherited from the women on my mother's side, they're spud-cut and a little lumpy. Inelegant.

In winter, these older girls carried out the tiring ritual of unscrambling themselves from their layers with remarkable grace. Delivering their long necks from circuits of wool scarf was, as ever, a site to behold. Like when an off-duty ballet dancer steps on the subway and everyone's head turns, influencing us to readjust our posture and perhaps reconsider our whole lives. Just like that, these older girls preoccupied me.

They were the prospect of fourteen. That summit age I arbitrarily picked, resolving it stood for what I now wonder might be a vacant pursuit: some cooked-up idea of *having made it* without divining what this unspeakable "it" marks or means. Or more humiliatingly, what it proves. When I turned fourteen, my sixteenth birthday newly assumed fourteen's folklore. Then eighteen. Followed by twenty-four. And so on, and so on. Recently, I've heaped extra faith into thirty-three's double springs; conceiving in its future roundness the calm of an absorbed, less wobbly world where I've developed a better sense of humor and experience with less acuity, the blow of life's ups and downs. Come thirty-three, I'll certainly valorize thirty-six. I'll reason it'll supply me with securities I have yet to fathom and eccentricities that permit me to slip out of my sensible mind. That I believe some big, whopping sign might one day parachute down and alert me to *my arrival*, is, I realize, foolish. Yet, here I am at twenty-nine, liberally investing notions of sureness into tomorrow's birthdays just as I did with those older girls.

Thing is, those older girls were on to something. They collected boyfriends in neighboring schools as if expanding the real estate of their allure. These older girls were wise to the curve and clout of their bodies in ways I'm still not, netting attention early in life when life was still framed by hallways and lockers, authorized by bells and permission slips, and upset by canceled parties or the turnaround caused by a new cut of jeans. They realized the one component critical for eternalizing yourself as myth, no matter what later letdowns or cruelties might come with adulthood: to never smile in photos unless it was the annual class picture. Pouting and appearing generally disentranced to the flash of disposable cameras was standard practice, but come picture day, their smile was athletically sincere. All at once obliging. I still remember most of their names—both first and last. They pleat my memory with singsong. Like the upbeat tempo of a 1-800 number.

It was as if I were standing in some figurative doorway with my head resting against the frame, watching these older girls get ready to go out: considering which earrings to wear, how to part their hair and do their makeup. Because observing any woman smudge shiny powder down her brow bone to her cheekbone, or flutter-blink her lashes between strokes of mascara, or delicately part her lips when lining her eyes—those rapidly precise, tidy-messy and pored-over motions—feels closest to catching a glimpse of her acquiring the world with quiet enormity from that faraway planet: her mirror.

It was the neighbor with the skinny-dipping daughters whose maple tree would blanket our pool with giant leaves and clog the filter. A pain in the ass to clean. The filter's round lid, which leveled with our cement yard, was—as if reminding us of summer's brief stint—permanently cracked. Backyard things have never appealed to me. Weather-worn white plastic chairs, flimsy-spongy cushions, benches with wrought-iron roses, ivy, and grape clusters that look, however modest, haunted or trapped in time.

Cursed, even. Backyards, for me, have either been fiction or totally spooky. There are few things more unnerving than when, in the dead of night, a backyard light motion-detects *something* but reveals *nothing*.

But my father's gripes with the pool were an extension of other presentiments, perhaps even imperceptible to him. Part of a greater pattern, like how he'd often point out while looking through photo albums that he wasn't present in any of the pictures because he was, customarily, the one taking them. The swimming pool and the pictures were both, in his way, father cargo. Drummed-into self-erasure carried out by someone whose experience of love seemed pending on another, unresolved lifetime, or raveled by how disorienting it is to find yourself skimming leaves from a pool on a Saturday morning when your daughter—who promised she would help with its upkeep—is instead inside, squinting at a television screen, refusing to wear her glasses that she too promised, for the price of their brand-name frames, she would wear.

Etched in my memory is the image of my father standing by the pool in his shorts, doing that thing he's always done: which is, *to assess*. The engineer in my father cannot escape his obligation to efficiency. Even in fatherhood, he's moored to logistics. It's what regulates that congenital disquiet I once thought was unique to writers but that I now see is shared by parents whose lives have been gratifyingly set astray by a gulch of worry and hope that comes with having a kid who one minute adores you and the next is grown and implicating you less and less. Because irrespective of how mundane a task, my father mulls over its mechanics until he's appraised the timeliest way to, for example, clean the swimming pool, mow the front lawn, and simultaneously prepare supper so as to serve the dal and rice hot—not warm—*hot*. So as to later enjoy from our kitchen window the pool's glistening surface at dusk while he scrubs and sets to soak the pots and pans.

But the look of satisfaction that warmed his face in these moments, that slid his glasses down his nose and ironed free the wrinkles on his forehead, was not mere fulfillment. It was far from it, actually. The meditative appeal of a swimming pool's evening reflection had little to do with how much work it took to create such calm but how, over time, my father had discovered that prosaic pursuits in a country he now called home eased the regret—that riotous, ill-boding strain of regret—of having never permanently returned *home* home.

As I witnessed very young, feeling favorably yet detached about one's life was a parent's province. To be wild about one's family while longing for the occasional interlude was inevitable because, for someone like Baba, the older he gets, the more disbelief about his everyday and deep ache for his own parents accrues. Unlike my mother, the act of missing provides him with purpose: reverence for what came before, for his roots, despite feeling uprooted. For his Jesuit school days at St. Xavier's, for so many friends from Jadavpur University—many of whom are long dead.

For those who are alive, whom my father can reunite with in Kolkata and tease. Isn't it lovely to tease old friends? To neglect the past's insurmountability and simply poke fun.

Striking up conversations with strangers, waiters, cab-drivers, and, in recent years, our dog, is, I've estimated, how my father both shakes off and communes with his ghosts. Unlike my mother, who does things in time—wonderfully exonerative time—who might peel two clementines and make a cup of tea before unpacking her groceries, who seems nourished, beyond what is normal, by some core system of replenishing ease, my father, like me, indulges, perhaps even self-indulges, in a sense of emotional hazard.

We're the types who keep from joining everyone outside, or rather, we enjoy-with-skirmish an autumn sunset's afterglow, anticipating instead the quick tide of darkness that comes next. Doom's ricocheting effect presses us and we're already back inside turning on lamps, commissioned by what feels intestinal. Still today, when afternoon light dapples and silver-streaks my stuff, exaggerating my pen's worth by extending its shadow across my desk or reflecting the right angles of my window in the round bowl of my wineglasses as they sit by the sink, drying from last night's dinner, even this sort of magic feels—I wish I knew why—somehow morbid to me. Perishable. Nobody ever teaches you how to be a person torn-between. How to shape your breaths so as to accommodate both the solitude and the stampede.

The morning we found the squirrel, my mother was

tasked with skimming the pool and retrieving its body because by then my parents had separated and my father was living nearby in an apartment, not far from the bowling alley where friends would throw birthdays. I was too young and selfish to appreciate all the ways my mother was now attending to things she had otherwise expressed no interest in prior to their separation. That she was also perhaps reacquainting herself with what I realize now were purely playful articulations of happiness—discovering a new shade of lipstick called Brick, for instance, which she still wears today, or reclaiming from her closet a cropped silver jacket she'd only ever worn on holidays but was now throwing on because, for whatever reason, Wednesday called for a cropped silver jacket. Back then, these adjustments were somehow threatening. Extremely suspect. My bad attitude was burgeoning and that silver jacket was aggressively *too festive*.

I was angry. Noxiously rude to any man my mother spoke to. I gagged with great effect when they'd ring the doorbell and relished how defenseless they seemed when taking off their shoes in our house, standing somewhat uncomfortably in socks.

I was a pest with very little patience for anyone who seemed laid-back around my mother; anyone whose baritone would carry from the kitchen to the second floor; who'd thumb through our CDs, crack open a case, and assume any of us were interested in listening to the Beatles.

It was around this time the word *idiot* lost its funny. I'd say it with my teeth clenched and something wicked. I was a girl upstairs in her room with the door closed, growing hostile. Impenetrable and uncertain. A combination that only seemed to accelerate matters and freshly renew my sensitivity to other families, mostly white, and their mountain-topped superiority. Their pantries with ready-to-eat snacks and incredibly practical junk drawers with seemingly no junk; wrapping paper and various colors of ribbon—new and spooled instead of recycled from old gifts. In my mind, these families were an avatar for goodness. Well-organized thoughtfulness. My envy churned thick since I wasn't yet teenage, and happening upon the translucent blahs that arrive with those years.

More and more, my mother's colleagues from the college where she taught were around, *in our home*, casually resting their hands on surfaces as they talked and laughed. Folding their jackets over the backs of chairs, leaning against our banister with one leg propped on the bottom step, and noting after using the bathroom, the spiced, earthy smell of our Mysore sandalwood soap. They somehow managed to occupy space in largely inconspicuous ways that drove me mad.

At first it was strange to hear adults I didn't know say my mother's name: Dolores. Their delivery had a tone I attribute to the formal informality of colleagues. Duh-*lore*-iss. Proper but acquainted. Or with a trace of French Canadian: Do-lo-riss. These colleagues knew her and saw her in ways I never had. Proctoring exams under the fluorescence of classroom light, carrying her lunch in re-cycled yogurt containers to department meetings, stapling flyers to corkboards and frustratingly unstapling flyers that had, she would recount later at home, covered hers. These colleagues' experience of my mother felt in breach of my own; destroying in some twisted and greedy manner my claim to her. They were privy to her nerve, and worse than that, they were probably providing my mother with support. Why did anyone have to know what was happening in our family? How did they know my name or what grade I was in? Why was anyone talking about me at all?

More so, why did they have to spend time in our house, where the mood was perceptibly changing, migrating away from the gloom of a marriage lost to, in retrospect, the gentle warping I associate with joy. Even our vestibule's Mediterranean-blue walls, where I'd kick off my shoes on terra-cotta tiles and hurry to the kitchen or my room—those walls appeared plusher. Like blue velour. The house was, once more, in possession of its many textures. It no longer felt like a shell.

Still, I was ashamed of having parents who'd fallen out of love with each other. Though it isn't mine to privilege, their separation was my first heartbreak. My voice began to, at random, condense into a chirp, signaling tears. Quiet panic sloshed around inside of me like stormy waters, and for a whole year, mysterious stomach cramps would come for me in the night, like gremlins conspiring in that part of my gut I hadn't yet distinguished was where I store secrets and where I hope dumb choices don't clot, and where I encounter—here, I'll say it—intermittent clairvoyance.

As a result, I began to worry nonstop about that which I couldn't control and, more so, knew nothing about: like money. When I needed some, for, I don't know, a ticket to see *Titanic* at the Cavendish Mall—again—I made a point of keeping tabs on whom I'd asked last. Because, quickly, my life required vigilant upkeep. Because, for some kids, when parents separate, the discreet incursion of agonizing about money or time spent, or learning to love just as much but showing it twice as much, of classifying belongings like photo albums or sets of plates, a teal vase, falls on the child whose inaudible awareness of adult pain undergoes what I experienced as a new charge. So, I strained to uphold a sense of equal. I developed a self-styled commitment to *what was fair* as well as nervous habits like pinching the cupid's bow of my top lip or folding my arm behind me and pushing my fingers against the beads of my spine; the latter of which I still do.

But while I withstood those bumps, while I was angry, anxious, and at times embarrassed to be the child of parents who sat on opposite ends of the gym during my ballet recitals, I was also occasionally none of those things. I had preadolescence to contend with, which in its way felt like a highly radioactive time where I was vying with myself for a sense of self.

In the ensuing years, I had all but decided my childhood was over. I never wanted to be young again because

I'd never truly felt the liquid energy of youth pool around me. Its alleviative qualities. This next period was marked by a dramatic break in how I thought. Or rather, how I started to plait my thoughts and overthink. And not as I'd done as a kid, fancying intricate scenarios through the slits of my neighbor's fence, expecting miracles, mystery, creeps of skin. No. Now I was reacting to how the air between two people can communicate heat: how a boy could make me feel midflight. Illegible attempts were sanitized by how, at that age, titles and sensitivities amount to little. How timidity needles redundancy. Did he look my way? Was that a kiss? Was it not? Did it count? Is he or isn't he my boyfriend? Do I like him? What's there to say over the phone? How do I fill the silence? Happily discerning cluelessness from the slippery ledge of being complicit has never been my strength.

One winter, as some friends and I walked home in the snow, sliding our boots like skis on the slushy sidewalk, a boy I'd grown more and more attracted to ever since I noticed how he'd lope up stairs, two at a time—sometimes three—or how hard he pushed his pencil into his composition books, stopped me as snow whirled down and as everyone else crossed the street. He leaned in and kissed me. His lips were soft. Mine were chapped. Our cheeks were cold. I was so taken aback that I covered my mouth with my wool glove as if muffling my *Wow*. I sensed all over my body the jolt of something unanticipated happening to me; of someone else's impulse pressed against my lips.

How even the most innocent acts swarm with pleasure because our nerve endings, thank goodness, never mature. Never mellow. They remain *prone-to*. Tendrils that keep us—in the best way—shatterable. Wasn't it lovely, I thought, to be caught off guard by the boy whose every mannerism I'd crystallized? Who I never anticipated was considering me.

But just as quick, as if being disallowed the phenomenal seconds that follow a kiss in the snow, I tasted a fleecy tuft in my teeth. Wool from my glove in my moment of *Wow* had hooked onto my braces. I felt sabotaged. When the boy tried to kiss me again, I backed away and kept my lips closed. I imagined the fuzz in my teeth looking like mold growing on my mouth's metal wires. Mortified, I stared at my boots and felt the wreck of inexperience, like a curse, condemning me to even more inexperience.

A week later, I sat perched on that same boy's top bunk, reading a magazine with my best friend, and needing to pee but too afraid to climb down—too scared to be seen climbing down a ladder. That certain scrutiny that races through you when you are bum-first and focused elsewhere— climbing into a public pool, down a bunk bed, up that rickety ladder to catch a rooftop sunset. When you fabricate, maybe, the burn of attention despite proof. When suddenly having an ass, no matter how flat or small, makes you feel immobilized.

From my perch, anxiously ignoring my bladder push against the round button of my jeans, I watched as the boy placed his cat inside an empty brown pillowcase. He proceeded to swing it like a pendulum, faster and faster, and then whip it around, whirlybird. "I play this game a lot," he told us, smiling. "She doesn't mind." That poor cat, I thought, but said nothing. That poor cat that was being launched in the dark, confused and scared.

That evil boy. That whole display of unfeeling; of complacency's cruelty. Shame was a scorch, and my immovable, self-conscious self, who so desperately needed to pee, was instead staring at this boy torture his cat. I tasted the fuzz from my wool glove—the memory of it—and felt helpless again. Displeasured and stuck like an anticlimax; like a candy bar jammed in its vending machine coil. I'd forgotten about the kiss but remembered in its place how natural it was for me to feel wedged.

Beyond boys, this period was also marked by regretful decisions, some never to be repeated. For one, I heinously overplucked my eyebrows. Looking back at pictures, it's as if I had vandalized my own face with a thin-tip Sharpie. My eyebrows were reduced to faint wisps, weird and bowed; obvious gaffes, crooked like filaments. My smile, subsequently, photographed deranged. Two hewed mistakes floating above my eyes.

Some other decisions were more prescient. I began to misinterpret my friendships with girls in my class; assuming a mutual bond where, in effect, all we were doing was sharing secrets and using them as our metric for closeness. If she knew everything about me, then we were best friends. BFFs. Forever and ever. Keepers, not of each other, but of the privilege we derived from knowing. We were each other's vaults, misplacing our longing or encountering it as boredom. We pried. We made pacts. Intimacy wasn't only affection but advantage.

Funny how in adulthood, the opposite is sometimes considered true. Nowadays I spend time, in excess of it, wondering about my friends—about our folds of perception: "Does she know that I know?" A secret she's keeping, for instance. Or news she's not yet ready to announce. Or the way an unkind thought about someone we know might pass through her mind between bites of roast chicken; that I won't press her to share, because I've likely had the same thought. Our innermost selves become, over time and out of love, a universe of nonverbal prompts. Those free clues we call inklings. A vague intelligence for speaking without saying anything at all. Or maybe with age we become more paranoid. Less vulnerable. Regulated by what's unspoken and, in turn, reluctant to delve. Maybe our connections form in tandem to us laying brick and mortar, building emotional walls that eventually surpass us.

Often it happens naturally, and a relationship I feverishly jumped into discontinues. Whatever gave rise to our correspondence—a season, it's possible, like summer's wine-laced inanity and our insistence on walking far in flimsy shoes, or the quickening that flows from connecting over some zeitgeist thing, like a book about women and solitude, like that tapas place with cheap food and red tablecloths—has dried up. Or maybe in adulthood we are more inclined to ration intimacy than carry it around like a trophy to give away intact. Our unreason and instinct miraculously combine, and loving her means also trusting that she'll share, if need be, what needs sharing.

Though I'll never know if I was ever perceived as an Older Girl and by whom, my memory of those years, of what was appealing about those white girls, is less and less absorbing. Less silvery, and nearly impossible to conjure. I was so young and so spellbound by movie beauty and so vulnerable to magazines. To the way magazine girls with freckles had *figured it out*: beauty that was somehow boyish, I reasoned.

It's taken me a while to reshape many of these notions because I was then, and still am, a late-to-bloom girl. Expectant like a card trick. The girl who for years wore a sports bra as her everyday bra, and would wait for the bus practicing my Liv Tyler pout, badly wishing for even a shred of her courteous Liv Tyler cool.

During my first session, five or six years ago, my therapist lightly amended a declaration I was making, with the words *For now*. The revelation was immediate. A tonic. Like when clouds part outside, and inside fresh beams of light reinstate the day—those six letters marked a huge shift. Because, as girls, we held on tight to Forever. It was compulsory: the most critical, tender quota. *For now*, however, is a far more rational unit of measurement, and perhaps one we should encourage much earlier in life because it doesn't require the insurance of a necklace or bracelet, or any token really. It connotes nuance and the balm of receptivity. It has little to do with girlhood's insistence on wide-eyed hopes for the future, or feeling like an easy mark, and, in my case, ceding so much power to those older white girls. What *For now* proposes instead is the give and grace of compassion.

Ick, ick, ick, my mother said, still wearing her nightgown and wrinkling her face at the dead squirrel. I glared, irritated. *I knew we were going to be late for school.* But from my window, as I watched my mother delicately retrieve the dead squirrel, it occurred to me that the squirrel suddenly looked saved. The droop of its body in the blue net, like the droop of a child faking sleep, slyly hoping to get carried out from the car and into bed. Drooping, I understood, was a kid move. Was this dead squirrel a kid squirrel? Still new to the world and unaccustomed to the spring of its bushy, plumed tail. Had it drowned while playing with a buddy? Chasing each other up the maple tree or across the telephone wire that stretched from our house to the alleyway where Joanna, Marisa, and I felt teenage long before we were teenagers because we were hanging out in an alleyway.

Maybe the squirrel had tried, in panicked and walleyed horror, to climb out from the water only to scratch its claws against the pool's smooth, rounded edges. Shaped like a kidney bean, our pool looked borrowed from Bedrock City.

Prehistoric, retro, like nothing we were used to. The sort of passed-down aesthetic I found alien and luxurious because the pool, like the whole house, had touches of what I considered the most movied place: midcentury Los Angeles. A "Mamie pink" and black-tiled bathroom, for instance. A lavender one too, with his and her sinks. Carpeting in most rooms and sliding louvered closet doors.

We never repainted or redecorated, save for that Mediterranean-blue vestibule my mother insisted on, and later, mango-orange in the downstairs hallway because, I'd venture, my parents figured out, perhaps soon into the move, that their marriage was in that stranded stage of an ending where temporary fixes—in this case, buying their first house without making it theirs—suspend ineludible pains.

Mostly, it bought more time. For my brother and I to delight in what makes a house remarkable: its sounds. Its index of noise. The discreet swish of my father knotting his silk tie in the morning. The panting steam of our iron. That one broken window and its frightening guillotine-drop. Mustard seeds popping in oil. The front door's particular key-turn. The back door's spring. If I close my eyes and sail back to our house on Wilson Street, there's one CBC radio program in particular—its plaintive opening theme—that may as well score the journey. There was too the thud of dropping who knows what upstairs, and how strangely, no matter what *it* was, the thud invariably sounded the same: like an unscrewed brass doorknob falling two feet and rolling over once. My parents would yell from downstairs—not *Are you okay?* but simply our names. Yelling from downstairs was without a doubt the most movied novelty. Like families in holiday films who speak over one another during meals, who reach exaggeratedly across plates, elbowing the youngest when grabbing the gravy boat and outing someone's recent breakup. Whom I couldn't help but sentimentalize solely because, of all things, they interrupted each other.

There was also the FilterQueen. Hard-to-reach corners of carpet in our living room meant hearing the brown R2-D2 vacuum butt against bottom molding. My father recently informed me that that vacuum was one of the most expensive items my parents ever bought for the house. He also added, surprising me with this next detail, that he and my mother nicknamed a close family friend of ours "Filter Queen." Apparently this woman had made a habit of spinning the truth meddlesomely in her favor.

When my father texted me those two details, I considered scrapping this essay entirely. The thought of my parents investing in a vacuum cleaner was somehow too depressing. Too proximate to the dimming I associate with building a family that above all—above all anecdote and filial affection—must function day to day. Must vacuum, ration most luxuries, account for pairs of mittens, fix lunches with damp carrot sticks, fix fights before guests arrive, schedule predictabilities, and coordinate dentist appointments for two kids in different schools, while eternally I remember these words well: *Find parking*.

Dimming, I'll admit, might be the wrong word. Accurate perhaps, only as much as it's an entirely amateurish thing to say. I don't mean to sound punitive, just mindful of time passing not in days, years, gray hair, but with a better understanding of what went on behind the scenes. In the front-seat silence of two parents saying little on our way to dim sum—speaking, sure, but that's altogether different. Or in the kitchen at night when they assumed we were asleep. Sleeping, sort of, with my head pushed into my pillow, lying in my bed, which stood adjacent to our house's heating duct and its sound channel, where whispers reverberated with very little discretion for my mother's tears or the choked no-sound of two people waiting for someone to speak first.

Mostly though, the thought of my parents teasing a friend, speaking in code, calling her "Filter Queen"—even now, with both of my parents happily remarried—that image of them, near-rascally and light, pads my nostalgia. All of a sudden, the good parts chime. Beluga-whale watching in Tadoussac. That picture of my mother and me. She's wearing her russet-brown Nehru-collar vest. I'm wearing my bowl cut like a helmet of dark hair secured around my big head. Sitting on her lap, I'm a daughter full of *Why*s who need only turn her neck to ask them. I am safe having never felt unsafe. The water behind us, blue like a green lozenge.

I remember Saturday breakfasts listening to Astrud Gilberto; how her voice—diaphanous, unconcerned—seemed to waft through the house. "Corcovado" was a breeze. I'd fill my plate with greasy potatoes and sift the serving dish for those extra-crispy ones. My eggs would go cold. I was indifferent to fried tomatoes. My father would quiz me on my times tables.

There was also my brother's friends. Patrick, Matthew, Nicholas. There were two Matthews, I think. How his friends' names, and mine too remodeled our family's language. A coherency of extra characters that dotted our dinner chatter.

Two of those boys have since died. Occasionally their goofy laughs, their stammer and sweaty hairlines, reenter my mind. I hesitate to indulge despite only seeing fragments: the dregs of ripple-cut chips crumbing the bottom of a bowl; wet swimming trunks clinging to chubby thighs; the dangle of a dirty Band-Aid peeling off an elbow. Reestablished clearly is the first time I noticed the curl of a summer haircut growing out on the back of a boy's tanned neck. Or how the raised estuary of veins on a boy's forearm was unexpectedly attractive.

When I think of my brother's childhood friends, of the two who are dead, I become, in those seconds, not inconsolable but wanting for my parents. I am homesick. Parent-sick. Cousin-sick. Okra-sick. Sick for the perfume of our linen closet, for the block prints on bedspreads that ornamented my periphery as a child. That I'd trace with my fingers, authoring elaborate stories merely by fixating on the frequency of a pattern. On pinks that were once red or purples that faded to blue. I am sick too for running errands with my father, accompanying him to the shoe cobbler. The smell of Barge cement and leather intoxicated me. And then, after, to the bank, where the tellers were flirts, I thought. They reminded me of *Law & Order* ADAs. That variant of tall white woman beauty. Strong jaws. Skirt-suited. Cleft sternum bones in sight.

I am sick too for the sanctuary of a home with a piano that never got used; a mother whose pardoning mien meant dust collected and papers piled, and a stray baby shoe was saved. It sits on a bookshelf in her home; the way objects in museums are no longer objects but artifacts.

I am sick for those years when I was paying attention without purpose. When I was arranging stories free of import, and when my imagination could draw courage instead of warrant that I stay in.

I am sick for days of the week. They carried more meaning when I was younger. Nowadays dates are what are significant. We save them. Save up for them. Cancel them. Plan ahead while our calendars fill up fast and Tuesday, on its own, means little. I am sick for Tuesday.

I am sick for using change to buy lime popsicles. Sick for slamming doors to emphasize my temper. I am sick for not perceiving winter. For being unbothered by February's frost; what I now observe as twenty-eight days of sky reflecting street slush. A whole spectrum of gray. I am sick for packing a snowball but being too shy to throw it and so I'd carry it in the gloved pillow of my palm like a pet snowball.

I am sick for using small scissors to cut cardboard hearts; for gluing them on paper doilies and writing someone's name with felt marker. I am sick for cardboard and paper and markers, and the time it took to make things before gifting them. How the world subsides when you're carefully inscribing each letter of someone's name in calligraphy you've reserved for special occasions.

I am sick for my incorruptibility. Sick for believing. Sick for my body *before*. Before I'd ever noticed I was in possession of one. Before full-lengths. Before I knew anything about valleyed collarbones, a stomach's folds, smooth legs, small wrists.

I am sick not for innocence as merely asylum, but innocence as custom. After a rainstorm, amid the general chaos of a home and what still needed to get done—laundry, dinner, dishes—my mother would always remark on the smell. I am sick for the custom of my mother looking up to smell the gospel of wet ground.

I am sick for wearing orange. For those years when I knew nothing about the need to abide. When I smiled with my teeth.

I remember the cool touch of my mother's palm on my forehead before bed and how both my parents had a thing for my brother's and my foreheads. How they'd push my hair back and cup the top curve of my skull, and tenderly point to the chipped shape of a chicken pox scar dented into my nose. Briefly in those moments, my mother or father looked, all told, peaceful. Abundant with zero trace of the day's bulk. It was as if in their minds that smooth plane of skin above my eyes kept me small. Would keep me small and hold back time, so long as it never outgrew the size of their palms.

Because I doubt any parent is ever ready to part with his or her child's smallness. That beautiful delusion of believing the whole universe is compacted into a tiny frame. Thinking back, the deep well of love my parents have for their two children, the labor and restorative leisure of it, even if we've outgrown certain comforts and warred at times over life and where it's taken us; even if I go days without a consequential phone call with them and sound curt and ungrateful when asking for a favor; their love has never been—not once—hesitant. This much I know.

The morning we found the squirrel, I watched from my window as my mother balanced the net's long pole, using her whole body to dip it over and place the dead squirrel . . . where exactly? Near the rhododendron? Here's where my memory goes static. Here's where I wonder if maybe it was my brother who scooped the squirrel from the pool. If so, did he grin mischievously, threatening to hide the dead squirrel under my bed? Does it matter? Here's where I realize maybe it wasn't even a school day and I was simply mad at my mother for some crimped and fiery but unnamed daughter reason having to do with being a daughter with a mother. Here's where I worry that my recall is, in fact, some ramshackle excuse for recall.

What I'm sure of is the dead squirrel's body and how I can't unsee its dark brown corpse like a blotch of balsamic in our aqua-blue pool. That house, its backyard, the lilac bush, my green shag carpet, the older girls, the boys, the squirrel, still wind me up. Like omens I neglected, like apprehensions I would only later—much, much later— understand as how my body was, in its way, anthologizing my childhood.

3

Miserable

PRONOUNCED *miz*, as in *Ms.* magazine. *Uh* as in an expression of hesitation. And *rull*, as in rhymes with *dull*. In my family, when someone is miserable, we say *miz-uh-rull*. We say it like this because, as a kid, I couldn't pronounce the word *miserable*. The *B* sound eluded me. I couldn't push beyond that second syllable and form the last two: the *ruh*. The *bull*. It was as if I was encumbered by the word's very meaning; too dejected to complete it. *miz-uh-rull*, it turns out, was my very own, self-styled onomatopoeia. Whatever inextricable despair I was experiencing at the age of three, it outdid me.

Some babies, once born, remain unready. Despite our smallness we are in possession of a lair of apprehension, chambered in order to lodge how estranged we feel when someone, say, tosses us a ball. Or expects from us pure jubilation the first time we encounter a Slinky. As a child, a Slinky stalled on a flight of steps caused me acute stress.

The way it would cede to its coils—sometimes pause and appear to levitate—and then fail, abandoning all momentum. I couldn't cope with the suspense. In photographs, my little hands are holding each other tight, or gripped around my wrists like clamps. Concern, far beyond my scope, was compacted into me.

There's something about a distraught child that is instantly significant. She gets it: the world is often ten seconds away from tasting like cold french fries. The world can assert itself like a category-3 shitstorm of major letdowns, and minor ones too, which I've learned are harder to make peace with because they are somehow inexpressible. Averting one's attention; reacting unreasonably with no tools to recuperate; seeking sanctuary in the company of friends, who are also unprotected from feeling wrecked; mending on an empty stomach; experiencing life as if you're watching it from behind a shoulder-high wall—ducking when it's too much, peering over to discover more, both wise to and oblivious of everything out of view, rashly tossing your effects over the ledge and starting over with nothing. The illusion of nothing, that is. There's no suitable language for feeling adrift when on paper you seem all right. Arguing with yourself into becoming someone else is next to impossible. And then the world disappoints. And no amount of interpretative power could have prepared you.

Perhaps I'm still too young to have ideas *occur to me*. Perhaps I learn and then forget. I've Googled many times what poison ivy looks like and I still can't identify it. Perhaps

I'm still unready to conceive of a life entirely my own because I'm preoccupied with the quality of blue in pictures of my parents before I was born. At twenty-nine—that cusp, almost craning, turgid age—I so badly miss hearing, of all things, my father fill the dishwasher, precisely, just as he's always done. Or how he still yells into the phone when he's speaking long-distance, to an uncle in India. How expressions of deep love in Bengali somehow boom throughout the house like disagreements might in English.

And what about life's near-invisible blips: those private ones like an email from my mother at 9:04 on a Thursday morning. "Just saying hi," she writes. I know she sent it from her computer, in her study, sitting at her desk of papers where, I imagine, in order to press the ENTER key, she has to brush aside the corner of a loose page—maybe her class schedule or minutes from a meeting. My mother's papers are overgrown. A jungle. My mother's *Just saying hi* is meant and sent with every atom of her mother brain, body, heart. She misses me. A mother's lowercase *hi* is catastrophic. It's the apple grabbed from the bottom of a pyramid display. I hadn't meant to be hungover on a Thursday morning, and yet. The culpability that accompanies daughterhood—while it might fade over the years—never fully lets up. I'd estimate even, it reestablishes itself. A whole planet of worry that's working in collusion with that part of my gut trained to fear the absolute worst when someone leaves a voicemail or when a friend texts "K."

When I search the word *miserable* in my inbox, most of

the results are from friends who've had colds. Who were writing to say, "I can't make it tonight." Miserable, in these cases, connotes the purely physical. A runny nose and fever, a sinus infection. The morning after a bad bout of food poisoning. Miserable meaning a weakened state.

Then of course there is the quality of being a deplorable person. It comes up in my inbox with regards to men. Miserable men. In one email, I mention to a male friend how a movie I'd recently seen is centered on miserable men. I go on to complain that there aren't enough movies about miserable women, but I'm careful to distinguish how miserable women are fundamentally different from unlikable women. In the email I sound superior, as if I'm trying to impress this male friend, who I've now come to realize is perhaps one of the most miserable men I've ever met. I've since decided that miserable men, unlike miserable women, are, in fact, unlikable too.

In 2009, one friend uses *miserable* while Gchatting with me. It's a Monday and she's recapping her Friday night. My friend describes how she spent the night overcome with jealousy, having thought she saw her girlfriend flirting with another woman. My friend tells me how she felt "miserable and then crazy for feeling miserable." This, I've decided, is an excellent use of the word. Feeling miserable is, by nature, a spiraling condition. Almost antigravity despite its Eeyore gloom. It's a looping state with that touch of screwball. *Miserable*, I've decided, might be the most good-humored way to characterize being in a bad mood.

My father, however, uses the word *miserable* differently than anyone else. In an email from long ago, he worries, for instance, that my brother is making a "miserable salary." Or that the bathroom in the apartment I've applied to live in is "just miserable." When he writes, *It's your decision*, he means, *What are you thinking?*

In 2012, he keeps me informed about my mother's sister's cancer treatment. The chemo she's undergoing leaves her feeling, he says, miserable. When your mother's big sister feels miserable—the aunt who's made and custom-decorated all the birthday cakes for all the cousins, dyeing shredded coconut and piping buttercream roses—there's really nothing to be felt, because your entire body becomes a wound. In the hospital, in bed, not wearing eyeliner or her glasses, she probably looked lost.

It's clear to me when my father says *miserable*, he means it in a way that makes me wonder if I learned it, all those years ago when I was buckled into my OshKosh overalls, from him. If you've ever had a sad parent, then you've grown up learning how to perceive sadness when it's being expertly concealed from you. When it occurs merely in how someone needs to conjure spare strength for basic tasks like pushing his arm through his winter coat sleeve or needing to sit at a slight remove from those other parents huddled close on the park's bleachers during a match. You've not so much witnessed sadness but sleuthed it. You've absorbed it, and, without understanding what it is, you might even mimic it. You've acquired a capacity for providing conciliatory silence. So silent even that one day on the way to work, my father, who every day dropped me off at day care before heading to the office, completely forgot I was sitting in the backseat. When he pulled into his parking spot and turned off the car, I said, "Baba, no day care today?" He turned around and gasped.

When I consider the context, there is a measure of charm to this piece of my childhood. *Miz-uh-rull* sounds less like an adjective and more like a collective noun. Like a miz-uh-rull of stalled Slinkys. Of wet basset hounds. Of empty seats, front row. Of stale restaurant rolls. Of introverts at orientation. Like a miz-uh-rull of Knicks fans. Or a miz-uh-rull of tossed Christmas trees on the sidewalk, well into January. A miz-uh-rull of—they can't help it—tuba players. A miz-uh-rull of tents in the rain. Dogs during fireworks. Delayed passengers at the gate. A miz-uh-rull of self-help books in the "Free, Please Take" pile. A miz-uh-rull of tangled necklaces. A miz-uh-rull of boarded-up storefronts by the beach. A miz-uh-rull of friends at a party listening to Whitney—she gets us moving, she's voltaic, a flash storm in D major—only to abruptly and quite mutually all feel the wrench of *Wow*, she's really gone. All of a sudden, you're a miz-uh-rull of friends listening to Whitney Houston.

The other day I was FaceTiming with my father and stepmother. I can't be sure what we were talking about, but it was evening and I was sensing, more so than usual, the current of daughterhood. It sneaks up on me when I can spot in the background, perimetered by my screen, their umbrella tree, for instance, and how it reinvents them, outside of me. Living their routines, watering their plants, going about their days. The phone will ring at theirs and it's Ray. Who is Ray?

After we did some catching up, I could tell my parents were about to turn on the television and watch the news, so I said—though it wasn't true—that I was meeting a friend. I pushed my face closer to the screen and waved like a maniac to suppress those tears that aren't tears, exactly, but a warming of my face, because my body reacts disobligingly, and confounds *goodbye* with just *bye*. Though I'd hoped to say, in jest, in some wimpy grown-daughter way, how this evening I was feeling vaguely miz-uh-rull, the call was already over. They'd pressed END, and the rude slight of my face was reflected back to me. How is it that coming upon one's likeness, *my own face*, can feel like an unsolicited affront? Vulgar. A harsh blow, not just to my vanity but also to my personhood. My screen-lit contours— somehow soupy—and the blunt quiet in my apartment were, momentarily, impassable. Those seconds that followed the call were a miz-uh-rull of seconds. A reminder of how damning *too late* can feel.

4

Gone!

I WAS seven years old, missing my two front teeth, and slowly recovering from a self-inflicted haircut that, looking back, produced a fantastically witless smile in pictures—a lunatic glint some of us harvest briefly in childhood—when one afternoon, someone stole my fish.

We were an hour southwest of Montreal, where Lac Saint-François, a tributary of the Saint Lawrence River, streams. And where if you're quiet, you can still conjure the sound of traffic. Sort of. Close enough for city kids to get wowed by a dragonfly's spangled wings; to feel the itch of tall grass and knock our knees on the pebbled sides of a cooler while carrying it from the car to a picnic table, as if being reminded how awkward we become when we are an hour southwest of our home.

It was me, my brother, my father, and Mark, our close family friend. If I recall, he'd just returned from a fishing expedition in the Yukon, or maybe it was nearer, like the

Quebec-Ontario border. Mark is an outdoor photographer. Or is it outdoor with an *s*? The outdoors. The numerous, ambiguous outside. He's also an actor, and one summer— the one my family met him—he was a counselor at the YMCA day camp I attended, teaching drama. I must have come home and gushed, describing him as "so cool," and "really nice," and "*soooo* funny," because soon my father and Mark became friends. Eventually, they started working together on projects, writing scripts and putting on plays with the theater company my father founded.

When my parents separated, Mark found it hard to stay neutral, I think. He was my father's friend and collaborator after all. And anyway, these situations are too involving for everyone uninvolved.

But just like that, and as I witnessed somewhat amazed, when my parents split, a far bigger parting occurred. An entire social circle divided. Some friends, not Mark, were particularly awful and self-important about picking sides. How often I heard those words: picking sides, choosing sides. To settle the unease that had since become my constant attendant, I resolved that it was a dance. The "pick-sides." Like the fox-trot, like bhangra, the jive, a waltz. The pick-sides was, plainly, a variation of ballroom tango— head-snaps, staccato steps, operatic turns. Footwork that mimicked all the talebearing and, in some extremes, slandering that these adults who frontiered my childhood were now involved in.

During the 1998 ice storm, when a chain reaction of

collapsed transmission towers shut down the entire city for a couple weeks, Mark stayed with me, my brother, my father, my grandmother, and my now stepmom, Lisa. One night, the fire alarm went off in my father's apartment building and Mark and he carried my grandmother down five flights of stairs in her wheelchair. I remember watching their arms buckle and my father's brow sweat, and his pants slide down his waist just enough so that instead of being helpful and hurrying in front to open the emergency door, I was telling him I could see his underwear. *Baba!* I shouted. *Pull up your pants!* Even worse, my grandmother was panicked and mumbling what sounded like prayer or distress—it was hard to discern between the two—and all I could focus on was how, without hot water, I hadn't showered for days.

Even the day we went fishing—five years prior to the ice storm—my attention was selfishly turned inward. How this was possible so young still startles me. On our way to the river, I remember feeling humiliated by Mark's enthusiasm for the day. Here we were, a father and his two kids who know zilch about fishing, accompanying this pro. Anytime Mark shared with us what he was looking forward to, how special this spot was, or what kind of fish we might catch, I grew more and more ashamed of how inadequate we looked in the adult-sized, mesh-lined fishing vests he'd lent my brother and me. How utterly foolish and useless one could look in badly fitting water-repellent gear.

Watching Mark turn around in the passenger seat and passionately go on to us as my father drove was—though of course no fault of his own—embarrassing for me. Even very young, I was aware of how inclusion, no matter how warm, alerts me to further ways I might need to catch up. Though Mark was just trying to be kind, all I could focus on was how I grew up in a house where nobody ever owned the right shoes for participating in activities like hiking or camping. Like, whatever you need for cross-country skiing. We had to borrow. We knew nothing about sleeping bags and building tents. I've never owned a fleece. And now of course I'm smiling because the last thing I ever want to do is climb mountains or push tent poles through grommets and worry about overnight rain. I find myself deeply hostile, even, toward the word *activity*.

When we reached the river, it was colder than we'd expected. I was shivering and got bored, quick. My rain boots were too big, so I felt—again with the clothes—stupid. After lunch we agreed it might be best to head home early, fish or no fish.

Just a little longer, my brother proposed. He's never minded waiting. So long as it doesn't involve waiting for people. My brother is patient for snow to melt, for meat to cook just right, for scars to heal. But people. People drive him mad.

I asked if I could sit in the car, knowing full well the answer would be no. All I wanted was to be inside. All

I wanted was a window to look out from; the swath and sound of water, faraway and hushed. All I wanted was some remove. On most days, that's still what I want. Because I've always enjoyed watching people I love do what they're doing, but from a distance. Far enough so that bodies become blemishes but that a person's gait remains familiar.

There's something peaceful about the tunnel acoustics of a car when the engine's turned off. It's what I imagine we hear before we die. Or perhaps it's those same acoustics capped by what I can only describe as the swift suction of a penny being vacuumed. Yes, that's it. That's the sound.

Anyway, my father insisted *we all*—including me is what he meant—try to catch one fish. It didn't matter how small. Few things bring him joy the way cooking fish does. He'll say it's because he's Bengali, but I know it's also because he derives great pleasure from what demands method. Where there is a system and where he can pride himself in not just using but owning the right tools: the right knife with a curved blade, the right pan, the exact spices, enough lemon. Even the act of eating fish requires care: *Look out for the bones*, he'll warn between bites.

While I complained, Mark remained cheery, because what's there to do with a family in a mood—a family that's not yours. He must have made a joke, because I remember letting slip the slightest grin that betrayed the frown I was so focused on wearing. Normally, I was fairly committed to my tantrums. I could stare down a brick wall. I must have thought Mark was handsome.

Despite wanting to leave, I grabbed my fishing rod and stood on a bed of raised rocks and began to count, because what else was there to do? I counted seagulls flying. Children in the distance, older than me. I counted the teeth in my mouth with my tongue. I counted how many days until Christmas. Until my birthday. And how old I would be in the year 2000. I counted down from one hundred and wondered about my best friend, Ali. She was probably not fishing, but instead eating sugary cereal and watching a movie with her German shepherd, Pêche. Or maybe then it was Hobo. Pêche came after Hobo. Ali's the friend whose phone number, parents' names—Andrew and Patricia— her pets' names, street address, color of her second-grade backpack, and Halloween costumes are all foundational. She was my first Diana Barry, even though as a little girl, oddly enough, I connected to Matthew Cuthbert more so than Anne.

As I stood on the rocks wishing I was elsewhere, imagining what fourteen would feel like in the year 2000, I felt a *yank!* Isn't that how it goes? When you've become a brat and cursed the day's activity, when you're bored and cold, and your boots are too big, that's when you feel the most violent *yank!* All of a sudden my line began to shake. The rod bowed and lowered in what looked like pain. I'd never felt tension so strong before. It was as though I'd hooked a magnet the size of a baby elephant. Or woken up a monster. I must have screamed, because Mark came running and took over.

I felt special. I stood back and watched as he wrestled with the line, leaning back and keeping the slack out. This went on for some time, and now my father had joined us. My brother too. I remember Mark focusing hard, talking to himself and to us, and enjoying the fish's fight. Water splashed; I saw a tail. Some wriggle. I thought about where I'd look if Mark lost the fish—probably the sky. Maybe my boots. I still don't know where to look.

Abruptly, as if he'd been pretending the whole time, Mark quietly reeled the fish in with plain ease. Like it was nothing at all. Thrilled, the four of us agreed to stay out longer. But first, Mark took a picture of my brother and me holding our catch. It was gooey and slippery and, to my surprise, very, very heavy. I smiled my lunatic smile, and a few months later, that same picture ended up in the pages of a Canadian fishing magazine.

To preserve the fish for dinner, we found a quiet area off to the side of the river and built a miniature fort with rocks surrounding a pool of water. A custom basin. In my memory, the rocks are bluish. Like if gray had a cold. My father expressed some concern because my lips had turned purple. But I was too focused on building a sturdy wall and playing too with these plastic, wormy baits that flopped and bobbed in colors like neon pink, yellow, pylon-orange. One worm was transparent and speckled with glitter. In a few years I'd wear a retainer with a similar coat of glitter that I'd eventually lose on a soccer field. My mother would make me walk the length of the field back and forth, but we'd never find it.

Once the fort was safely built, Mark gently slid the fish inside its temporary home. "Good catch," he said. "Are you sure you've never done this before?"

We left the fish in its basin, walked away, grabbed our poles, and hooked new bait. For the rest of the day, whatever we caught was to be set free.

A couple hours later, we returned to the tiny stronghold we had built. It took us a minute to find it, but when we did, the fish was gone. Someone had stolen it. "What?" my father said. "Impossible."

I was devastated. Mark wondered if we'd perhaps walked to the wrong spot. My brother didn't seem bothered in the least. The wind picked up as it does when no one is in possession of an appropriate response. It was time to pack up and head home.

As we hiked back to where our car was parked, I put my hand in the vest's side pocket and accidentally pricked my finger on a lure's hook. There was no blood, though it hurt enough for there to be blood. I turned around and arched my neck to mark the spot where we'd left the fish. Even from far I could see our fort, and just beyond that, in the distance, I noticed a couple wearing matching turquoise windbreakers. They seemed nice enough—I mean, really, there's no telling. I was seven and missing my two front teeth, and slightly suspicious of the world, especially now.

But something about those matching turquoise wind-breakers. They provoked me, and if anything, they've stayed with me. No billowing, no sag. Those turquoise windbreakers fit perfect. They ticked me off. They tipped me off, and in that second, I decided: *It was them.*

5

The Girl

THE girl you want does not exist. Despite agreeing to split two entrées and seeming, in your eyes, charmingly frazzled by the menu's options, her favorite time of day is *not* dinner with you. Her favorite time of day is when the waiter starts coming around with his tray of votive candles.

She picked this place for its big booths because they make her feel like she's sinking into a giant baseball mitt. Sinking into a hug. She only accepts hugs from furniture. From the throw cushion she places on her stomach and holds tight, like a soft fender for her gut. From the way her mother doesn't look up from the paper, doesn't say *Good morning*, but instead, "I thought I'd let you sleep in."

She accepts hugs too from the weight of a dentist's X-ray apron. From a rack of checked coats like a curtain she can fold herself into. From going to the movies alone in the day. From resting her face against cold marble surfaces.

From listening to her dog sigh. From Stevie Wonder singing low, *That I'll be loving you always*. From stepping into a patch of sun and closing her eyes.

She is standoffish, unwilling, harsh, up to something. She is a narcissist, a snob, a spy, some suspect. She is haughty, selfish, plenty vain, and proud. Affected. She puts on airs, I've heard people say.

She picked this place too for its wall-length bistro-antiqued mirrors. Even when she's looking at you, she's looking just beyond you—at her reflection.

Despite your grievances, she isn't withholding. Simply, she'll never tell you the things she takes an interest in, because what she doesn't want is this: that you procure them for her.

You yearn for her vulnerability. Which you believe comes complimentary, like peanuts on a flight; two packets. Like a smile. Vulnerability she refuses to give you because she is, after all these years, gaining back custody of herself. Lost long ago, before she was born, somewhere in the ripped lining of a purse where, I assume, most things lost will eventually be found.

Hers is an everyday process of retrieval. In general, she moves at the speed of someone gathering dirty laundry from her floor—bending down, scooping up, yanking socks from jeans, inspecting smells, discovering tears or a stain she'll deal with later. Regretting a brown cardigan she only wore once; the buttons were all wrong, but she knew that when she bought it. Slipping on heels she'll only wear at home. Getting distracted by a ticket stub in a pants pocket. That's the speed she moves at.

She isn't one for accomplishing anything fast. She's too sensitive to accomplish anything fast. Even her thoughts come out like goop from a tube. Like those Sunday hangovers—her brain nodding and floating like a bouquet of delivery balloons wrapped in plastic.

What absorbs you though is merely *her*. Your obsession is your obsession. You've been encouraged to believe since boyhood that your fascination has manifested her. She is an iceberg you've mistaken for an island. Discoverable in your eyes.

She is open in ways that do not attract attention in the same manner *she* attracts attention. There is a difference. And neither requires your sanction. One is private while the other occurs when her joke lands. Or when she extends her neck and communicates her posture. Like when a copper penny is dropped into a vase of limp tulips. Within hours, the tulips look spry. Standoffish, unwilling, harsh, up to something.

The girl's life forces include, in no particular order: pleasure scored from what is incomplete; a firm belief that procrastination provides charge, builds muscle, helps to— over time—discover register; tenderness for people who arrive places in a panic, sip fast, are in possession of fail-safe exit strategies.

She wishes she had a genius for curbing small talk; for manufacturing an arbitrary tone when airing something considered; for soft-boiling an egg.

She always feels like a tourist the morning after she spends the night; after she leaves your place and experiences the glare of sidewalk. Like she's meant to be going to a museum, so sometimes she does. Like she's meant to be ordering a pastry. So, often, she does. An espresso too—those small to-go ones she can cup between her thumb and index finger. Like she's meant to be a woman who wears sunglasses. But she's never worn sunglasses. Not once in her life. So she doesn't. But she feels like she could, and that's the point. She feels like a tourist whenever she has sex.

She has trouble sleeping. It shows because people tell her it shows. Those dark, deep-set half-moons that hammock under her eyes invite appraisal. In pictures, her mouth is slightly open as though she just said *Tapioca*.

It still isn't clear to her what turns her on. Though just recently, while going for a walk, she spotted a stranger's pale rose curtains from the street. An early-summer breeze sent them flapping out the window only to get sucked back in, clinging against the building's outside brick like the thin skin of collapsed bubblegum. The flapping. The clinging. The sucking-in. This turned her on. Or maybe the spectacle was, simply put: intimate. Belonging to someone else. A person she would never know, whose entire room on sunny days is stained pink when the curtains are drawn. Walls blushing. Inside looking like insides.

The girl sometimes confuses what's intimate with what turns her on. You like this about her. You love that she is confused. You lean into the table and tell her, adoringly, "I can't believe you exist." The construction of your praise troubles her. It's your claim to her, after all. Is that your best offer? Your disbelief? The whole display, like most displays, is a small dog wearing a top hat and monocle. It's a gift you expect her to open in public. Because recognition of this kind is humiliating for both parties. *Taking notice*—if one isn't cautious—is smug. Chaffing. Tedious.

"I can't believe you exist," you repeat.

While inured to this variety of compliment, she would like nothing more than to climb out from behind the scrim and roll her eyes to the point of migraine. She wants to bark. Shake the ground. Grow tentacles. Swing on a chandelier. She wants to hide. Disappear. Become a speck.

Tell a woman she is beautiful, and she might—it's very possible—feel like a fool. Roses die quick. They will do.

The girl you want does not exist.

The girl you want does exist.

But not like that. And not like that. Or like that. Or like that.

She is sitting across from you, looking just beyond you—at herself.

6

Idea of Marriage

Y dad's idea of fun," my friend Tait once told me, "is having a few drinks and then telling either me or my brother how beautiful his wife is." Tait's mother, Sandy, is very beautiful. Elegant. She speaks with steadied attention and just enough breaks between her thoughts, like someone rummaging through her purse for a pen. Some women sound as if they are working through their ideas out loud, open to doubt but not impaired by it. Some women hand you a pen before you even ask for one. Sandy is one of those women.

She looks nimble and ready for whatever; capable of contorting her body like a woman from Robert Longo's Men in the Cities series. In fact, if I remember correctly, Sandy was one of the women Longo depicted in charcoal and graphite. Makes sense.

It doesn't surprise me that Tait's father's idea of fun is

telling his two grown sons how beautiful his wife is. What entertains Tait's father, at least as Tait tells it, is Sandy.

But more so, what I've always enjoyed about that anecdote is how Tait expressed it to me the first time. The construction of his telling. How Tait chose to describe Sandy not as his mother but as his father's wife. The indication being that his father was speaking about marriage, about his wife, Sandy, and the woman in the Longo, and while he was speaking to his two sons about their mother, he wasn't.

7

Moby-Dick

PLOWING through *Moby-Dick* my senior year of college, I found a reading chair in a well-lit corner of the library where I could sit uninterrupted for hours, readjusting my posture at various times, convinced that with each redistribution of my weight on one leg, one side, I might experience improved focus. I was chapters behind, having procrastinated the previous two weeks' readings, and now, here I was, confined to the library, tucked beside the main stacks, desperate for a friend to walk by and distract me or suggest we stroll to the vending machine for Peanut M&M's.

The day progressed. The library's quiet came to be its own noise. Like artificial silence forged from real silence. Sham silence. Like everybody in a library is playing pretend—which in college is not entirely untrue. But isn't that often the case inside spaces where quiet is enforced? How the absence of sound produces a sonic texture in and of itself?

I considered leaving at one point because reading so much, so closely, and not merely for pleasure is deranging. Sentences begin to float off the page and my focus becomes unfaithful, and the book starts to flop like a fainted body.

As daylight waned and disappeared, and the air inside felt wired, I nearly dozed off. I'd read a couple hundred pages and decided that after this chapter, the book's eighty-seventh—"The Grand Armada"—I'd stop. In this chapter, the *Pequod* discovers a pod of many whales, including several pregnant female whales. Some have just given birth to infant whales, and are nursing them while surveying the *Pequod*. Like planets with eyes.

The "little infants" are described as "frisky," having scarcely recovered from that "irksome position [they] had so lately occupied," writes Melville, "in the maternal reticule; where, tail to head, and all ready for the final spring, the unborn whale lies bent like a Tartar's bow." Their crumpled fins are likened to a newborn baby's ear, and at one point, Starbuck notices how one young cub is still tethered to the mother's umbilical cord. Long coils of it. A "natural line" snared with the *Pequod*'s own rope.

I'm reading and imagining the umbilical cord, and the cub, and the mother, all of it, in "that enchanted calm which they say lurks at the heart of every commotion," and I'm picturing the satiny surface of the sea, how it's dark and blue as if promising rare secret moments like this to happen in its shadowy depths, and I finish the chapter and look up from my page and then down at the library's carpet beneath my feet, and there, coiled and dragging, is a cord. Lengths of it, looping and alive. Winding. Tangled. The janitor has started vacuuming. The library will soon close for the night.

8

D As In

URGAN. Jerga. Durva. Derika. Durgid. These are just some of the names people have misheard when I introduce myself. I rarely correct them, having long been convinced it's easier this way. Easier in the totally yielding sense of the word, as if being impartial about and casually erasing my most essential self—my name—complies with an imaginary code I've lived by: that establishing room for everyone else is the quickest route to assimilation. My mispronounced name was, I'd fooled myself into believing, *how things would always be.* Like that one button on my winter coat that I'm constantly sewing back on. Or how I'll never be someone who knows any jokes. And so, at twenty-eight, I'm still skittish with my own name, fumbling during first meetings as if "Durga" were a bar of wet soap.

At Starbucks, I'll place my order and tell the barista in an apologizing tone, "Just D." Nobody has time for that back-and-forth lingual dance of me repeating my name only to inevitably spell it out: "D as in Dog." But "Just D," that's my escape: the speediest way out of everyone else's way. "Just." The word connotes impartiality but also scarcity, and in those moments, another acknowledgment of *how things would always be.* "Just," as in "Hardly D," or "Not quite D." "Just" as in *barely there.*

The same goes for when I make a reservation or greet the hostess at a restaurant. "D's fine" is what I'll say in a slack warble as if unencumbering her. Most times though I'll give my friend's name without the slightest hesitation, because mechanically disallowing my name in favor of what I assume is more commonplace has, over the years, become reflex. "Table for two under Fiona," I'll say spryly. No sweat. Sometimes I feel miserable doing that, like the pangs I pocketed as a kid anytime I couldn't reconcile my parents' Indian heritage with my own Canadian childhood, but mostly, I rarely notice my impulse because it's just that, chronic.

Mindlessly self-deleting, it turns out, is addictive. And while these little accommodations have simplified some experiences, there is the gamble that my willingness to write myself out of my daily encounters will curb the potential for A Tremendous Me: big goals, big wants, and dreams I've left in the cold or crystallized. I've often wondered if my friends whose identities have meshed more seamlessly with the world, who've never had to repeat their names in line for a coffee, say, are more readily encouraged to occupy ineffable spaces too. Like their future, or the load and levity, both, of ambition.

There's a type of inborn initiative that comes from having never been obligated to answer questions about the meaning of one's name, or one's country of so-called origin, or to explain that the way you look is generationally and geographically worlds apart from where you were born. Since childhood, there's been an assumption that I owe strangers an answer when they inquire about matters I myself struggle to have words for, let alone understand. When it comes to my identity, the ways in which it confuses or interests others has consistently taken precedent, as if I am expected to remedy their curiosity before mediating my own. In this way, I've caught myself disengaging from myself, compromising instead of building aspirational stamina. While uncertainty about my future is of course not unique to me, I do marvel at the bounty of hesitation I have acquired over the years because I surreptitiously presumed potential was a dormant thing; that it only functions as a trait others see in me.

One response has been to blend in. When I was very young, I used to have a running tab of Indian names that were, I perceived, not so Indian. That could pass as what, I wasn't sure. All I knew was that they seemed more *accessible*. Anita was one of those names. Kiran too. Looking back, this kind of quiet yearning was not something that preoccupied or pained me so much as it was an element of some deeper and unmined sense of disorientation: that

I am first-generation and, in turn, proficient at splintering who I am in order to accommodate everyone else's environment. I'm in awe of people who appear immediately comfortable on a stranger's or new friend's couch because I am the friend who is always encouraged to take off my coat, to "make myself at home."

To be first-generation means acquiescing to a lasting state of restlessness. It's as if you've inherited not just your family's knotted DNA but also the DNA acquired from their move, from veritable mileage, from the energy it took your parents to reestablish their lives. I grasped early—perhaps one February morning as I warmed my feet inside the car while my mother scraped snow off her windshield, her rosy cheeks emerging through icy diagonals on the glass—that my parents were not from here but from there: Kolkata. There she was, removing snow with great purpose and rhythm as I spasmed with chills until I was toasty and warm. There she was, my Anglo-Indian mother, Dolores. She from *there* but now living here, wearing winter boots and a puffy coat. And me, her daughter, who is from *here* but also, in some conveyed manner, from there too.

That distinction is one that accompanies me every day but one that I have been careful to never overly indulge. What tethers me to my parents is the unspoken dialogue we share about how much of my character is built on the connection I feel to the world they were raised in but that I've only experienced through photos, visits, food. It's not mine and yet, *I get it*. First-generation kids, I've always thought, are the personification of déjà vu.

While in some ways my name is one of the smallest kernels of who I am, I now know that something far more furtive is at play when one's name is misheard. The act of mishearing is not benign but ultimately silencing. A quash so subtle that—and here's what I'm still working out—it develops into a feeling of invalidation. Nothing will make you fit in less than trying, constantly, to fit in: portioning your name, straightening your hair, developing a wary love-hate fascination to white moms whose pantries were stocked differently than yours, who touched your hair, admiring "how thick" it was.

Swapping between the varied pronunciations of my name had its effect too. When I was growing up in Montreal, my French teachers would sputter the *D* with a tsk, and at home, my father's Bengali accent would round the *Dh-oor* sound. In my mind I always imagined his articulation written in felt marker; in bubble letters. But the North American way of saying my name is the one I've come to know and use. *Durrrr-gah*. Like the hum of a machine capped by the gleeful sound a wiggling baby makes after knocking over her bowl of Cheerios.

The first-person essay is not one that comes naturally to me. Who is this "I"? Am I entitled to her? Is she my voice, or is she the voice that is expected of me? One editor has urged me to claim the "I" instead of exhausting my rhetorical crutch: "One might say . . ." When I have a point to make, I'm tempted to sideline it or deceive myself of its ownership. To delight in anonymity. The way I see it, these admissions are everyday to anyone who was born accommodating—who's read enough "I's" in enough essays but has never seen "me."

To want and to write in the first person are two actions that demand of you *you*. But this long and lanky "I" has never arrived at me freely. How can an "I" contain all of my many fragments and contradictions and all of me that is undiscovered? Is this "I" actually mine to own? If you are someone whose first-self intrigues others, writing in the first person necessitates that you grow fascinated with yourself.

The very desire to *write it all down*, to trust that my experience and what I might share of it has merit, is a foreign prerogative. Often, I'll be thinking aloud with friends or deliberating on ideas that have been simmering or, on luckier occasions, ideas that have been connecting, and a friend will excitedly chime in, "You should write about that." But the impulse to *write it all down* is at most secondary or tertiary, and generally not even on my radar. "Everything is copy," Nora Ephron famously said. While those three words inspire, in my case, being held accountable for a voice that is perhaps not my own but is inferred because of my name or the color of my skin can be stifling. My first inclination is to let ideas sit. To overthink and wrestle with them. To feel outpaced by them. Or grow impatient with this odd affair I have with writing. And then maybe, just maybe, I'll draft an email to a friend where I blunder the original purpose of my note: to seek out a single-person audience.

And so at twenty-eight, here I am working hard to un-learn. A couple years ago, my friend Sarah and I followed a group of friends to a bar after attending a panel orga-nized by a magazine we've both contributed to. At some point a guy approached us and asked our names. "Sarah," she said. I followed, only to be asked what I've now deemed the token follow-up question: "Where are you from?" Before I could answer, Sarah snapped back at him, "Why would you ask her that?" Sarah's barbed inflection when she delivered her *you* and her *that* entirely delegitimized him. She not only rebuffed his question but the entitlement he'd likely subsisted on his whole life, unchecked. I was mortified at the time. It's possible I recoiled into the collar of my coat. *Sarah! Really?!* We were new friends, and her sharp takedown of this stranger seemed unjust to me. Briefly I thought, *Poor guy.* That is, until the next morning when I woke up feeling light and unburdened.

Those few seconds in the bar were a revelation. Ever since I can remember, it's been customary that I arrive somewhere, anywhere—a party, a new school, an interview—with a tagline or tributary anecdote, like a note that I've tied around my neck with yarn. "Where are you from? What does your name mean?" Those two questions have been asked of me so many times that I respond with a singsong cadence, as if rattling off my address when I order Thai over the phone.

My preparedness with new encounters has always been in the service of others, so much so that I wouldn't even call it preparedness; it was just *how things would always be*. But after that night when Sarah spoke up, everything changed. I recognize the dramatic nature of pinpointing change to a single seemingly insignificant event, but I've also come to realize that some shifts should never be backtracked, because the only person you'll end up devaluing is yourself. Since that evening, a newfound and speedy confidence sprang up in me like a cartoon flower in bloom. I am now awake to the undermining agency and the chain reaction of everyday reticence such questions imposed on me. *Thanks, Sarah. Love you.*

I now too recognize the absurdity of people who can't be bothered to pronounce my name properly but are willing to straightaway request I tell them where I'm from. Their othering of me depends, it seems, on their capacity to other. It's usually those same people who roll their eyes when I say I was born in Canada, who reiterate "Where?" as in "Where *where*?" like I haven't heard them the first time. A life of this farce is sure to sand down anyone's sense of self. And maybe that's the point, to bolster one's power and belittle someone else's: mine.

After years of my pleading, my mother finally gave me her yellow-gold *D* ring that was passed down to her from her mother. Daisy, Dulcie, Dolores, and now Durga. The ring's band is thinning so I don't wear it often, but when I do, I feel the clout of family. Few things yield such command. I'm from somewhere! And these women had something to do with it! The weight of those two facts is, as I grow older, increasingly humbling. With that lineage comes the consideration that if I have a kid, I should perhaps give him or her a *D* name. But what? Should it be Indian? How many Indian *D* names do I know? These are the sorts of thoughts that slide through my mind in the morning when I've been in a long-term relationship, when I've considered my future, seriously and unseriously. These are also the sorts of thoughts that cross my mind when I'm out at a bar and a stranger asks my name and where I'm from. And as I impatiently play with the ring on my finger, I wonder, *Do I really want this kind of dim encounter for my kid?* But then I feel the embossed gold lettering, the most capital *D* I've ever seen. *D* as in Durga, Dolores, Dulcie, and Daisy. *I'm from somewhere!* I'll be reminded. *And these women had so much to do with it.* I am an accumulation of them and myself, and have a newfound vitality born from no longer accepting that I am an accumulation of my misheard name, no longer inured to self-evasion, to ceding my totality.

9

Since Living Alone

1.

I LEARNED last summer that if you place a banana and an unripe avocado inside a paper bag, the avocado will—as if spooned to sleep by the crescent-laid banana—ripen overnight. By morning, that sickly shade of green had turned near-neon and velvety, and I, having done nothing but paired the two fruits, experienced a false sense of accomplishment similar to returning a library book or listening to a voicemail.

There is, it's worth noting, a restorative innocence to waking up and discovering that something has changed overnight. Like winter's first snowfall: that thin dusting that coats car rooftops and summer stuff like park swings and leftover patches of grass. Or, those two books that mysteriously fell off my shelf in the night, fainting to the floor with a cushioned *thump!* I place them back where they belong, pausing to stare at their bindings, which

I've memorized, if for no other reason than when you live alone, the droop of plant leaves, a black sock poking out of my blue dresser, or an avocado that ripened overnight—all this stuff provides a rare, brief harmony: the consolidation of my things, all mine, in a space fit for staring off as I skirmish with a sentence on my screen or wait for water to boil. The only person who might interrupt my thoughts is me.

2.

"When you travel," writes Elizabeth Hardwick in *Sleepless Nights*, "your first discovery is that you do not exist." This sentence, which I read in late September as I shuffled and flopped from my couch to my bed and then back to my couch again, chasing patches of shade as the sun cast a geometry of light on my walls, this sentence surfaced on the page like a secret I'd been hurtling toward all summer but, until now, was nothing more than a half-formed figment. (I've come to hope for these patterns that build in increments, eventually sweetening into an idea I've long been blueprinting in my mind; I've come to understand them as a huge chunk of what writing involves.)

While reading Hardwick, I noted that since moving into my one-bedroom apartment in late April I had traveled little, declining invitations upstate or weekends on Long Island or in Pennsylvania. I chose instead to stay put. To seek the opposite of not existing and acclimatize myself, it turns out, to myself. Even writing those words now feels like a radical act because a large part of who I am has always hinged on someone else. I am a daughter, a daughter of divorce, but with my own stubborn and cautious interpretation of what that means. A child that never quite reveled in the traditions of childhood, a younger sister and her eventuating appetite for the sentimental, for the Beastie Boys, for asking "What did you eat for lunch?" when what I meant to say was "I love you."

I was also someone's girlfriend and, subsequently, the emotional commerce of being someone's ex-girlfriend, or the person whom you write emails to at two in the morning, or the person you might expect to dislike, or the person who finds herself stuck between a plant and a kissing couple at a stranger's party.

I was a roommate to three people and a cat, a roommate to one person and two cats, a roommate to someone turned sister, forever.

I was the loyal friend but also the girl who never answers her phone but who will text back immediately: *sorry. everything ok?*

I was the witness at your wedding, who took a tequila shot with you before City Hall in a bar full of midafternoon men with bellies. They all swiveled right, in unison, as we walked out. You in silver-plate heels and me in black linen overalls.

I was the woman whose shoulders are too bony to lean on but whose thighs have cushioned his naps in that hour on Sunday before dinner when the hangover has worn off and the sleepy sets in.

All of these relationships, crucial as they were and are, accelerate involuntarily. Being Someone's Someone is cozy in theory—a snug image like two letter *S*s fitting where the convex meets its concave. Unfortunately, I felt little of that snugness. I'd sculpted myself into what feels nearest to apparatus, a piece of equipment that was increasingly capable of delaying my desires. There was always tomorrow, I told myself. There was always next semester, or spring, or the uncanny extent of a summer day. Or winter. *Or winter*, she says. The most fictional of seasons because winter is lit for the most part with lamps and candles and, in some cases, the arbitrary oranges of a fireplace instead of the natural brightness, say, of the sun. Winter's wheaty indoor amber glow emboldens the bluesiest approach to oneself, which is by nature the easiest to deny. But repudiating the would-be is a quality that many women can attest to no matter the season, because from a very young age we were never young.

I can wiggle my way into small spaces. I'm more flexible than I appear. I sleep in the fetal position. I do everything in my power to stifle a second sneeze, and if that fails, I apologize mid-sneeze. Because I have a low pain threshold, I seem to have developed, as a reaction, a high tolerance for the swell and plummet of other people's moods. And so I whittled myself away because—and this is where as a writer I duck and cover—I've been for most of my life confusing the meaning of words. I've confused privacy with keeping secrets, for example, and caring with giving.

3.

In the past my response to conflict was, by some means, bogus math. Prescriptive as though the advent of apology was, I was convinced, my first move. Figuring myself into the equation would come second because I had disciplined my definition of "relationship" into rationale. *Ensure he feels proud of his work before you can focus on yours. Read little into what she said last night; she's having a hard time. Listen. Listen better. Master listening.*

But living alone is the reverse of mastery. It's scuttling around in surrender while hoping you don't stub your toe, because living alone is also a series of indignities like bouncing around on one foot, writhing in pain. Living alone is an elaborately clumsy wisening up.

Since moving into this apartment on the fourth floor of a building just one street over from my previous place, I regularly trip over things: shoes, computer cables, the leg of a chair, and of course, ghost things too strike. Just yesterday I placed a clean pot back on the top shelf of my kitchen cabinet only to have it slide back out and conk me on the head with such aggression that when I yelled *FUCK*, everything went silent: my buzzing fridge, the patter of rain on my air-conditioning unit, the slow and sped-up metronomic tick that resides inside of me and competes with my heartbeat for what really compels me. Any vain attempt to expect jokiness, for instance, from a pot that mysteriously falls on my head no longer exists. Since living alone, grievances occur in silence. Deep and shallow thoughts court and compose me like deep and shallow breaths.

4.

As someone whose central momentum is *having connected*, similar to the high of *having written*, my life before living alone was, to exaggerate, one very long practice session. I'd been avoiding myself with such ease that even when an obstacle presented itself—like the pained limits of a friendship that had run its course—my response was to adapt around it the way we circle street construction on our way to the subway without much thought, as if the ball and sockets of our hip joints, anticipating those orange pylons, swerve so as to save our distracted selves from falling into crater-sized holes.

Avoidance can be elegant, certainly, because elegance, like restraint, is a spectacle that assuages. Even the word—*avoidance*—smooth as if meant solely for cursive's sleek lines; a speedy unthinking gesture like one's signature.

Edmund White once wrote about Marguerite Duras in *The New York Review of Books*: "Her work was fueled by her obsessive interest in her own story and her knack for improving on the facts with every new version of the same event." In less than thirty words, a tally of four *her*s.

I count living alone as, in a manner of speaking, finding interest in my own story, of prospering, of creating a space where I repeat the same actions every day, whetting them, rearranging them, starting from scratch but with variables I can control or, conversely, eagerly appeal to their chaos. I can approximate what time it is on sunny mornings by glancing at the frontiered shadow that darkens on the building adjacent to mine, casting a crisp line that cuts the building's sandy-yellow brick, lowering notch by notch as quarter past six all of a sudden becomes seven. It takes me fourteen steps from my bed to my bookshelves and nine steps to walk from my front door to the globe lamp I've propped on a stool under a wall I've half decorated, of which a poster I've framed hangs asymmetrically next to nothing more than blank white wall. That globe lamp is the first light I turn on when I return home. For nine steps when I walk in at night, after shutting my front door and placing my keys on their hook, I navigate the slumbered mauve and moonlit darkness of my space. It welcomes me, the darkness.

5.

Living alone, I've described to friends, is like waking up on a Saturday and realizing it's Saturday. That made-up sense of repartee with time. Abundance felt from sitting upright in bed; the weight of one's duvet vanquishing, by some means, all accountability. Rarely traveling for half of last year and staying in my new place all to my own was similar to the emotional pluck those first few sips of red wine supply, or from riding the subway after seeing a movie; riding it the length of the city only to forget that this train rises aboveground as it crosses the East River, suddenly washing my face with sunlight or, in the evening, apprising my reflection in the train's window with the tinsel of Manhattan's skyline.

Precision of self was a quality I once strived for, but since living alone, clarity, I've learned—when it comes—furnishes me with that thing we call boldness. Self-imposed solitude developed in me, as White wrote about Duras, *a knack for improving on the facts with every new version of the same event.* Living alone, I soon caught on, is a form of self-portraiture, of retracing the same lines over and over—of becoming.

There's just one problem. Nothing catches me off guard quite like suddenly—sometimes madly—seeking the company of someone else.

In those moments, loneliness imposes temporary amnesia. How did I end up here? Had I lectured myself into some smug and quarantined state of solitude? Was living alone analogous to the emotional moat I construct around myself whenever I listen to one song on repeat, again and again?

Becoming is precarious terrain, and in spending so much time on my own, I had perhaps developed in solitude an acute distrust of myself. Seeking, I've since learned, is okay. How many women, I wonder, caught off guard by an unexpected stream of tears, have walked to their bathrooms and glanced at their faces in the mirror? A brief audit: dewy eyes, flush cheeks, damp and darkened bottom lashes that cling like starfish legs, but mostly the way my face, shook by *what is happening*, to the daze of unforeseen peril, finds solace in all the inexplicables that on some days come at me with suggestive force. I am a daughter, I remember, with parents whom I can call. I was once someone's girlfriend for those formative girlhood-spun-sovereign years, so that's surely something I've carried. What else?

I tend to forget or, rather, rarely cash in on the proximity of people. If I wanted, I could walk a few blocks and find a friend, a friend who is likely experiencing coincidental gloom, because if there's one thing I know to be true about New York friendships: they are intervened time and again by emotional kismet. Stupid, unprecedented quantities of it. We're all just here, bungling this imitation of life, finding new ways of becoming old friends.

6.

There's a painting by one of my favorite artists, the Swedish painter Karin Mamma Andersson, titled *Leftovers*. In it, a woman is depicted living in her apartment, occupying the space in five separate moments of time. Sleeping. Dressing or showering, it's hard to tell. Sleeping once more. Washing her face. Going out. The space has the meticulously worn character of a stage: set-designed attributes like a lone chair, blouses flopped on a coffee table, and the miniature dollhouse-like synthesis of square footage. In this way, *Leftovers* reminds me of my apartment. A collection of stuff, all hers.

Parsing Andersson's painting was, for one summer, a pastime of mine because I had chosen it as my laptop wallpaper. Staring intently at this anonymous woman's space, her camel coat and mustard floor lamp, her bathroom sink—too low, as most bathroom sinks are—I began to endow her anonymity with qualities of my own. These are the games we play as women because, since birth, interior spaces have been sacred; have been where we imagine furniture mounted on ceilings or marvel at the weight of curtains and fabricate for fun what lies behind them.

Perhaps she too leans against her kitchen sink in the morning as she sips coffee, worrying without right *about everything*, or cruelly and quite shamefully envisioning the funeral of someone she loves. Perhaps in living alone, she, like me, experiences self-voyeurism, self-narration, self-spectatorship more sharply than ever before. Doing domestic things like the dishes or dumb young things like ordering takeout while perhaps still drunk the next morning. Both versions of me, since living alone, have settled into a one-woman show that I star in and attend, that I produce and buy a ticket for, but sometimes fail to show up to because, as it happens, living alone has only further indulged the woman—me—who cancels a plan to stay in and excitedly ad-libs doing nothing at all.

And yet, I'll still attempt pursuing these delusions in spite of reality's firm hand, in spite of that which keeps us indoors: money, panic, books that lay in piles near my Nikes, books I absentmindedly begin reading instead of tying my laces and walking out the door.

7.

The first thing I ate in 2015 was a pear my friend Katherine left at my place on Christmas Eve. The pear, brown and stout as if missing its neck, was a pear unused, spared from a dessert she had prepared for dinner that night. Something with cinnamon and whiskey and perhaps another ingredient. Lemon juice? Before leaving, she placed the brave little stray on a shelf in my fridge. It sat there for seven days and eight nights, wrapped in a plastic bag that clung to its coarse skin as if suffocating it. *Pears*, I thought whenever I'd open my fridge during those haphazard days that wane between Christmas and New Year's. *Pears should never be wrapped in plastic*. Paper, I concluded, is what suits.

It's likely this notion has something to do with *The God-father*, the second one, because one of my favorite scenes in the trilogy occurs moments after Vito Corleone has unfairly lost his job yet still returns home to Carmela carrying a pear wrapped in newspaper. He gently places the gift on their table while she busies herself in the kitchen, and in those few seconds I've always been taken by what I can only describe as the privacy of kindness. Those moments leading up to—that anticipate—the testimony of kindness. Kindness before it has been felt, before it, by nature of its mutual construction, even exists. Kindness at its clearest.

On New Year's morning, I woke up and placed a cutting board on my stovetop and sliced Katherine's pear in four fat slices that I then halved so as to begin the year with a sense of plenty. I stood at my counter and ate each piece as if I had intended to do so all along, as if I had waited all of 2014 to eat that pear.

That's the thing about living alone. Artificial intention blurs with real intention, and sooner or later, more choices than not—like eating a pear first thing in the New Year—seem decisive, so much so that even a pear can deliver purpose, and if you're lucky, peace of mind too.

10

Tan Lines

COME summer, my reluctance kicks in. It's as if the sheer persistence of a July day—the sun's glare, its flecked appraisal of pavement and trees, those bonus evening hours—solicits from me an essential need to withdraw. Thankfully, writing is an indoor sport. Sometimes I go stretches of days without much sun, and even in the swell of midsummer I maintain what could be characterized as my winter pallor. Though pallor might not be accurate. How might I describe my brownness, my very fair brownness, that following winter appears even more fair? What's the opposite of *glowing?* Dull? Drab? Run-down? Blah?

These questions are not as good-humored as they seem but are fixed instead to my tendency for self-scrutiny, activated long ago when I came to understand my sense of belonging—my *who-ness*—as two-pronged. The beautiful dilemma of being first-generation and all that it means: a reflection of theirs and mine, of source and story. A running start toward blending in among mostly white childhood friends who were rarely curious about my olive-brown skin, the dark shine of my hair, my chestnut eyes. We were kids, after all. We were one another's chorus, encountering parents—and the *elsewhere* that entailed for me—only in consonant environments: a birthday party, ballet recitals, rides to the movies in my parents' burgundy Toyota Previa.

In terms of family, this elsewhere—my parents' *who-ness*—was abundant yet imperceptible. It was my home. Where I ate and slept, and wore big T-shirts to bed, and watched TV, and played Parcheesi, and fought with my brother, and savored the leeway of a Saturday morning, and where I would get scolded for tossing my jacket on the divan, or be corrected for answering a question with "I don't care" instead of "I don't mind."

And, come summer, I reexperience with particular clarity these accumulations of a home, not merely through memory's piping but in actions. Despite New York City's stifling weather, how the air distorts into a muggy mass, I drink hot tea and eat hot soup. It cools me down. Because in that sly way science naturally alloys with what we inherit, I've been told since childhood that hot liquids provide remedial chill. This slight reprieve on especially sticky days, I like to imagine, is a discreet reminder that my parents are not always but sometimes right. That the knowledge they've imparted to my brother and me is not purely an expression of love but firm testimony of their own provenance, and how what keeps us close reveals itself not just in facsimile but, over time, in what kindly amounts in kernels. An everyday tip, a turn of phrase and its unusual construction, reminders to not sit on my bed with "outside clothes," for instance, or how in the summer my body yields to the season's balm with what I've come to regard as heritable agency.

Those beads of sweat that collect on my nose are entirely my Mama's. The annual, deep-healing effects of humidity on my dry skin; that's hers as well. If friends come over to my apartment and I offer them "some tea," those two words conjure my father's anticipant inflection on scorching weekend afternoons when he sits on our porch having proudly just fixed something without needing to replace it, like the broken nozzle of our gardening hose or the loose legs of a chair.

In my case, inheritance has never simply been what trickles down through traditions but is also the work required to disallow how those traditions fade. To recover the various genetic dispatches like those from my grandfather Felix, whom I met once, long ago, in Kolkata, in a kitchen, I think, of which I remember little except for the color green. A tablecloth, maybe. A moss stain on a concrete wall. Perhaps the whole memory is enameled green because for no discernible reason some colors naturally coat nostalgia with geography. India, for me, has always been protected in a layer of green.

There is also my paternal grandfather, whom I never

met, and his wife, my grandmother Thama, whom I did. And there is my other grandmother, who died when my mother was a teenager. Her skin was far darker than mine, a trait I noted as I studied one photo album in particular, confusing the musty scent of protective parchment sheets with what I imagined she herself might have smelled like. I remember foolishly wondering as a child if my much lighter skin was an outcome of brown girls growing up in cold climates. A discordance that epitomized how split I felt between life at home and life outside, overcome and enamored by my white friends and every so often experiencing waves of assimilation met by lulls of wanting nothing more than to seek lineage, move backward, claim the brownness of my skin as I only knew how: through family.

I became more aware of my skin, as most of us do with our bodies, in adolescence, and especially when summer arrived. Halter tops. Shoulder blades. Crop tops. Sweat stains. Denim skirts. Shorts. A growth spurt marked by how my knees now knocked my bike's handlebars as I pedaled to the park. The many ways we learned to twist and tie our T-shirts so they'd ride up our stomachs or whorl around our waists. Bathing suits. Boys. The convention of boys in the summer; how, suddenly, they memorialized the season. Still, I became heedful of the sun's currency on my body. The sun's signature on my skin and how the contrast of tan lines carried merit. That I was expected to feel virtuous was strange to me. I tanned fast. Brown to dark umber in a matter of hours. But what struck me was this:

it was as if my white friends were wearing their tanned skin—bathing in it—as opposed to living in it. The thrill of becoming temporarily dark was, for them, an advantage. It would take me a decade or so, longer even, to consider or be faced with what dark skin means in the world and how my relationship to my skin is further complicated by how fair it is and the access it allows me, and oh, what a luxury to be allowed a decade or more of girlhood in the first place.

The level of excitement among my New York friends, in the summer, has now hit a fever pitch and results in one thing: plans. So many plans. An incessancy of plans. An ambush of them, really. Unspent from winter's reserve, these nascent leisure hours develop into a vague inertia where we sip slushy tequila or inestimable glasses of rosé, or where I park myself on a roof in Brooklyn and characterize the far-away hedge of buildings as "a view," and where I squint at my phone or the same paragraph in my book and feel indebted to the car passing below blasting *that song*.

And let's not forget the beach. Here, among families and unaccustomed sounds like splashing water and seagulls squawking, we zone out, obscure the sun with shades and funny hats, nap in quick spells, signal over friends and scoot over to make room on our towels and blankets. Summer is many things, but it is, certainly, the season for scooting over. Plans and scooting over.

As new–to–New York adults, living here without history but with the audacity to claim space, these mini migrations from rooftops to small stretches of sand, to the fire escape at sunset where we climb out and gawk and attempt the impossible—to acquire the sky's display in a few inches of touch screen—somehow constitute *spending time*.

Now picture what happens when my skin tans. *When it doesn't.* When over the years my white friends have lathered themselves with Hawaiian Tropic and announced with a sense of crusading enterprise their plans to "sit out and bake." When they've spent long weekends at a wedding in Palm Springs or a house on Fire Island, coming back to the city with burns they bemoan, only to quickly and quite airily reevaluate: *Well, at least now I have my base layer.*

Trace back to high school and then college, when my white friends would return from spring break, from all-inclusive resort vacations or a week at their cottage. Without fail, the most common occurrence—one that has persisted through adulthood—is this: my friend will place her arm next to mine, grow visibly thrilled, and exclaim that her skin is now darker than mine.

The things I've heard: I'm *almost* as brown as you. I'm darker than you now. We match. I'm lucky I tan easily. You *look* like you tan easily. You don't even have to work for your tan.

I'll stop after these two: I'm basically black. I wish I had your color.

Since the average white person's spectrum of darkness is limited, the language of tanning is appropriative at best. Witlessness masquerades as admiration, co-option as obtusely worded praise. Compliments, in some cases, can feel like audits.

Growing up brown in mostly white circles means learning from a very young age that language is inured to prejudicial glitches. Time and again, I have concealed my amazement. The semantics of ignorance are oddly extensive and impossible to foresee. Close friends of mine goof. There is, after all, no script. As Wesley Morris recently wrote, "For people of color, some aspect of friendship with white people involves an awareness that you could be dropped through a trapdoor of racism at any moment." Zero notice met with my own long-harvested ability to recoup, ignore, smile, move on.

What leaves me uneasy is the covetous near-pricing of quick-tanning skin, so long as the experience is short-lived or euphemistic—a certificate of travel, a token of escape, time off. Proof of having *been away*. Like the watch you forgot to leave by your hotel bedside, that you wore to the beach as you dozed off at noon and then again at three— even that goofy tan becomes, for what it's worth, a holiday trophy. A mark, in some cases, of status.

As a kid, I accepted the compliments my skin would receive from, for instance, the mother offering me orange wedges after a soccer practice, or as I reapplied sunscreen at the local pool. I was, as most children are, innocent to the syntax of difference. How some obscure the act of othering with adulation. The luxury of privilege is so vast that praise is presumed to conceal bias.

But that was then. That was before I could place what was so upsetting to me about the mothers at soccer practice. The mothers at the pool who were looking at my body. Feeling watched yet accepting their compliments, and politely smiling, created a tenseness inside of me I couldn't yet parse. And anyway, it was hot, and the water was cool, and why were these mothers I barely knew talking to me at all?

I have two bathing suits. Well, two that I wear. A one-piece, navy. A two-piece, black. A couple of summers ago I was Gchatting with a friend as we both shopped online for new suits. Bathers, I call them. It must have been late winter or early spring because, from what I remember, we were typing in errant ALL CAPS, singular to anticipating a summer that threatens to never come. *Gonna FINALLY buy a bike*; *can't WAIT to not wear socks*; *I wish we knew someone with a POOL*. At one point she linked me to an all-white one-piece bather that scooped low in the back. *I could NEVER wear this*, she typed. *But it'll look SO good on you, especially when you're tanned*.

I've come to interpret comments like my friend's consideration of my skin, how it darkens in these summer months (first inside my elbows, as a boyfriend once pointed out to me), as plain enough. Depending on my mood, I regard or disregard them because I've grown up hearing, as most girls have: She is *this*. Looks great in *that*.

That my skin "goes well" with paler shades has never

discouraged me from wearing black, which I ordinarily do. My brown skin, it turns out, means growing accustomed to uninvited sartorial *should*s: You should wear yellow. More red, pale blues, and pink.

In the summer, my skin might bronze or redden and even freckle. It silhouettes my scars and turns sweat at four p.m. into liquid gold. But it might also, as if in defiance, preserve its paleness. On the brightest days, I go to the movies. Occasionally a museum. In bed, I sleep pushed up against the cold wall, or on the opposite side, with one leg dangling. For nearly five months, everyone leaves their windows open. Available to me are the season's many sounds. Even alone indoors, I am in the company of others. One neighbor is humming a song she was listening to earlier in the day. Another has started smoking again, cigarettes she never finishes. And another is on the phone; speaking to someone, that same someone, always, who I've long suspected must be mute. Sometimes I'll only leave my apartment once the sun is no longer hitting at an angle; when it's merely *there*, capable, reasonable.

But of course there are those days when I'm out, and it feels good. I return home in the evening, and my eyes need a few seconds to square with that interior grainy dullness. I'll catch glimpses of not just myself but my hands, and the length of my fingers: my mother's. Or how my cheeks, now ruddy, have rounded my long face, and briefly, there he is in my reflection. My father's smile. His father's jawline.

My brother's too. The manner of a person passed down in how the light sculpts a face and how shadows are not just cast but connect me to that framed picture of my grandmother when she was young. The sun still has hours before setting. My skin is warm. It does not cool. The heat is in the seams.

11

Summary Pictures

I.

I CALL them "the movies." Never indefinite—"I'm going to a movie"—but instead, a stipulated and familiar certainty: the movies. I do it, perhaps, as a nod to my childhood. To preserve my capacity for dupable wonder. Or possibly to modify, with the slightest article shift, the casual nature of going to a Cineplex; buying my ticket, a soda, some snacks, maybe; riding the escalator, and invariably forgetting what theater I'm looking for—was it nine or six? I choose to observe these steps as more than just a series of small, unremarkable transactions.

More so, characterizing it as "the movies" appeals to what I intensely crave, especially during summer's incurable groan: a sense of ceremony. A custom. An aggrandized, nonliturgical and yet somehow pious dark space where, despite the indignity, or gross charm, of sticky floors, the company of a snoring stranger, or the weak boom of a mediocre blockbuster, I experience the humbling feeling of being an audience member. Of succumbing to the emotional tremors of moving pictures. Of sneaking in fresh blueberries with my friend Teddy, and then, once the movie is over, riding the escalator to the next floor, and sneaking into another screening.

II.

Summer in the city is relentless. The sun is undiscerning and the days feel bloated and condensed. The presumption is—and let's be clear, summer is the most presumptive season—that being outside is compulsory because the weather tempts that side of us that is entirely coerced by rare commodities. A park with both clearings and shaded benches. The friend with a car and an afternoon destination. The bar with a backyard. A T-shirt at night. The private outdoor luxury of a balcony.

But seeking refuge from the heat is too an amenity that typifies New York's adhesive temperatures. A cool draft, however desired it might be, sometimes just won't do. I need more. A freezer to dip my head into. The subzero ATM vestibule of a bank. A precariously quick-spinning ceiling fan.

In this way, there is no sentiment more fulfilling in the summer, particularly since everything and everyone appears a little maddened by the scorch, than making a deliberate choice. Some stay from the sun but also the wakening warmth of emerging. Spend a few hours in a dark, icy-cool theater, and quickly the impact of ninety degrees invites me back into the world in a better mood. The throng of people everywhere? Not a problem. The blinding glint of pavement? I love it.

Because going to the movies still feels like playing hooky, or what I imagine playing hooky felt like: the unburdened act of avoiding my many orbits of responsibility. Of pretending that adulthood is no match for summer's precedent, set years ago when we were kids and teenagers governed only by the autonomy of no-school, the distance our bikes could take us, an unlit park or basketball court at night, the weekend my crush returned from camp. Going to the movies is the most public way to experience a secret. Or, the most secretive way to experience the public.

III.

I've never understood bliss to be an emotion one wears to a barbecue or encounters while sipping warm beer at the beach, but instead a measure of prosperity I can only feel in its truest form, privately. With a book I inch through, delaying its last pages or sitting in the company of a friend while she putters around her apartment reorganizing papers in piles and absently recounting a story from long before I knew her at all, much less as someone I would eventually love.

Summer movies, by virtue of their big gambits, impart

a similar sense of private bliss. I give into it. The more substantial the better. Surround sound that comes for me and threatens to forever doctor the rate of my heartbeat. That wallops and startles, and makes it impossible to discern between the dinosaurs before me and the rumbling inside of me. An epic love story told over decades that, without reserve, centers love as life's only piston. When two beautiful actors share a first look, confirming how only one of their characters will survive. Summer movies about big love are candy. Just like that, the running tab of things I have to do vanishes. The frequency of discipline and disquiet that skulks inside of me slackens.

The moment the lights dim and the studio logos run, I encounter a mix of my past swimming up inside of me as well as the true pleasure I derive from anticipation. Disney's "Wish Upon a Star"; MGM's roar; Universal's unapology, its trumpet and sun-eclipsing planet Earth; Warner Bros.' nostalgic piano and its gilded back lot and superhero lettering; Paramount's snow-peaked mountain; Columbia's Torch Lady, and so on and so on. These logos move me. They petition from me how crucial it is to preserve a sense of the special.

IV.

There was a contest in elementary school where the prompt was, if I remember correctly, to draw or paint an activity that illustrated how our families spend time together. We had a week to complete our work on an 8½-by-11 piece of construction paper. I still remember the fiber-like texture of the paper and how I was convinced I would win the contest. I went home that night and sharpened my Prismacolor set of pencil crayons and began to sketch with an industriousness singular to girls who were once praised, far too young, for being perfectionists.

On Fridays, my local video store had a deal on classics. A two-for-one thing that spared my brother and me, and mostly our parents, any arguments. One for him, one for me. He loved *The Great Escape. The Guns of Navarone*. War movies. I was partial to Audrey Hepburn. Our parents always insisted we rent the Marx Brothers. Some of my earliest memories of rolling around laughing, of physically reacting to comedy, I associate with *A Night at the Opera* or *Duck Soup*. My mother's head would fall back as she laughed, and my father would clap with sweet recognition, reexperiencing a scene he first saw two decades ago in Calcutta. My brother too, his big gummy grin widening each time Harpo waddled on-screen.

These Friday-night movies stood out as the rare occasion when my parents weren't fighting. It was important to laugh when they laughed, to try as I might in my miniature mind to prolong a marriage that was already, for what it's worth, over.

Scrupulously, I drew our basement. I mixed two shades of beige to match our carpet and felt the burn of pencil crayon between my fingers the faster I colored. I was careful to capture my father's beard exactly how he trimmed it and dressed my mother in lilac because it was her favorite, or perhaps with the cruel impulse daughters occasionally possess, I'd spotted a mother I admired wearing lilac and wished my mother wore it too. I drew my brother and me on the floor, lying on our tummies, our chins cupped between our hands. Smiling. Then, at the very end, I took an eraser and delicately smudged a pyramid of light emanating from our television and onto our faces. This detail, I was sure, would clinch first place.

A boy who painted his family sailing somewhere in Ontario won the contest. The runner-up was my friend who drew a scene from her lake cottage. There was a kite. A barbecue. A shaggy dog. It wasn't that I hadn't done a good job, my teacher assured me, but that she'd wished I had drawn my family and me outdoors. The beach was suggested. Or a picnic in the park.

But what I knew was this. We were happy watching Hepburn hug Peck on the back of his Vespa in Rome, or marveling at Kay Thompson singing her Vreeland-inspired directive, "Think Pink!" Or following Steve McQueen as he jumped fences on his motorcycle, or listening to Rita Moreno kick, and stomp, and dance her case for America, or giggling, as a family, whenever Groucho quipped. These moments, the movies, were how we spent time together.

Nowadays, I still enjoy peering around me midway through a screening. The blue light flickering and reflecting off of strangers' smiles or rounding with sinister effect the shape of their eyes. Each person's face becomes the moon. A theater filled with moons: halves and crescents, some full. I think back to how carefully I smudged the TV's glow on my family's faces. Less than a year after coloring that picture, my parents separated.

My father moved into an apartment not far from us. Once he was more settled, we began ferrying between both homes one week at a time. Always on Friday evenings, before or after dinner.

As summer descended, sweltering with little letup, I spent whole afternoons in our cool, dark basement, at what was now called "Mom's." As if pressed to trick continuity into my life, I started compulsively watching movies. Sometimes the same ones over and over until the tapes became too hot and the images and sound slowed. I'd persuaded myself that the only way to arrange time and, essentially, postpone how differently things felt upstairs was to devise a pattern of uninterrupted escape: Hitchcock, Bogart, Cary Grant. Hitchcock, Bogart, Cary Grant.

It seems obvious now, but I couldn't reconcile with summer's aliveness. How everyone was out and on their way somewhere, riffling through corner-store freezers for raspberry popsicles or peddling fast only to sail downhill, hands-free. I wasn't having any of it. I chose instead to live out my feelings through film, by pleading with Grace Kelly to not answer the phone—*Turn around!* I'd scream. *There's a man hiding behind the curtain!* Or mouth the words as Audrey Hepburn points to Cary Grant's cleft chin in *Charade* and tunefully asks, "How do you shave in there?" Or enjoy with great enchantment Peter O'Toole's slapstick charm in *How to Steal a Million*. His blue eyes, I remember thinking, were pure fiction: they were movie-blue.

V.

Going to the movies means securing a momentary fissure in time where I might cede to improbable bank heists, shit-out-of-luck heroes, to the very concept of a hero, to the winsome appeal of first love, star-crossed love, or an unlikely yet pleasing ensemble cast, a disappointing sequel, rapid-fire buddy-comedy banter, to the obstinate gloom of a boxing movie, a bummer car chase or a sensational one too, to the congratulatory thrill I procure from identifying voices in animated films.

When I exit the theater I feel smug with power having just stalled time. At least that's the lie I tell myself, because in my own misshapen idea of it, I have successfully suspended summer's most common emotion: longing. What it comes down to—despite having sat motionless for two or so hours—is being possessed by energy that I can only describe as kinetic.

12

Some Things I Cannot Unhear

1.

I N 1968, James Baldwin, a guest on *The Dick Cavett Show*, said, "As Malcolm X once put it: the most segregated hour in American life is high noon on Sunday." *High noon*, he said in a slight baritone, as if trying to find the right key for a song. Baldwin then went on to give examples of other institutions, not just the Christian church, where systematic racism has wielded its power; the labor unions, the real estate lobby, the board of education. Part of this episode can be found on YouTube and runs a swift one minute, one second. Baldwin's voice—its near-sport of a voice—is one I cannot unhear. The way he says "evidence" is capable of galvanizing the most blasé listener. His is a staccato that quickens in clip when Baldwin repeats words like "white" or "hate," but ripples when he says "idealism," diminishing its meaning into a naïveté.

When Baldwin asks a question, it does not ferry the

inflection. Instead, he issues it declaratively, testing the acoustics of a room. Close your eyes and, sure, Baldwin has a sermonizing tone, but one that bounces like someone hurrying down a flight of stairs without holding the railing. Baldwin's voice multitasks, and requires of me to pay attention. His words have carried their repercussive meaning into today, so much so that in August when the headlines read "No Fly Zone Over Ferguson," for a minute, I only heard those words in Baldwin's voice.

2.

My father has taught our two-year-old Welsh terrier, Willis, to "Play dead." PLAY DEAD, I'll hear him say when I'm home for a visit, sleeping in and playing dead myself. PLAY DEAD. Two words that I can now never unhear. PLAY DEAD; two words that oppose but aren't opposites. One is meant to be light: *Play!* The other is blunt. It moors.

When Willis hears PLAY DEAD, he lays flat on his side and possums into a jelled state. In those seconds, he is the ultimate state of "dog." Meaning, he is expectant. A treat is on his horizon. Sometimes Willis will side-eye my father, like, "C'mon, man." When a dog side-eyes you, the whites of his eyes can deploy more attitude than the most teenaged of teenagers. The most silent depiction of exasperation. A limit has been reached. The dog is *letting you know.*

And so, sometimes I'll stand on our stairs and spy my father saying PLAY DEAD, and even when Willis only half-obliges, my father stills hands him a treat and lies down beside him. In those moments my father is the ultimate state of himself: father first and everything else second. And in those moments when the two of them are playing dead, I quietly climb back upstairs because, as time passes and as I spot my parents doing young, lighthearted things, I'm overrun by some cruel and preoccupying sense that I'm watching the memory of them.

3.

There's a recording of Nina Simone's "Ain't Got No," where Simone, after listing all the things she doesn't have—a home, shoes, money, class, a country, schooling, children, sisters or brothers—she begins, around the two-minute mark, to list all that she's got, that "nobody," she sings, "can take away." Hair on her head, brains, ears, eyes, a nose, and her mouth. She has her smile too. Her tongue, her chin, her neck, and, my favorite of all, her boobies. When Nina Simone shouts "my boobies" in her syrupy, cool-wail of a voice, it's as if she's invented a whole new body part. Boobies. These aren't just breasts, they're boobies; they bob and hang. They're funny and beautiful. They're boobies. And I can never unhear Nina Simone claiming hers.

4.

I was eighteen and hiking with my classmates in Mexico's Copper Canyon when, while crossing a rope bridge, my foot broke through a rotten plank of wood and I plummeted thirty feet to the ground, landing on a dried-up riverbed of rocks. I don't remember falling—that was quick like something that didn't happen. I came to, and I remember the sensation of my tongue touching my gums and the taste of blood, and mostly the pain of vanity—I'd lost some teeth, it was clear. I remember the faces of my classmates rushing toward me and holding my neck and asking if I could wiggle my toes. I remember thinking, *lie*. Even if I couldn't wiggle them, I would lie. But I'm a terrible liar, and I remember deliberating on that too. These were my thoughts as blood trickled down my cheeks and as I committed to memory the faces of people I knew, whose faces now were stricken with panic. Warped worried brows and young eyes suddenly wiser because holding back tears will age you. Lips quivered and smiles cracked as I lay there answering questions—my name, the date, where I was—and as I learned by heart, as if studying for an exam, the way John's eyelids blinked slowly as if allowing himself a few extra seconds to look away from my busted face as he held my hand, or the way our guide spoke at a gentle metric like a robot with a heart.

The adrenaline that was pumping through me and masking my pain was also prompting my everyday discomforts to surface: I really did and still do hate being the center of attention. I'm no good at answering questions about myself even if they are basic and were meant to address possible head trauma, like, "Durga, what did you eat for lunch?" I stumbled on the word *sandwich* and couldn't remember if I'd eaten my apple or if it was still in my pack. Never before had I imagined that misremembering my lunch would yield such concern.

But what comes to mind most from that day is the sound that slipped from my mouth as my foot fell through the plank. It's hardly a sound and mostly a breath. A gasp that was cut short, as if sliced by a butcher's knife: it sounds something like *Huh*. *Huh* like the laziest reaction. Like a giving-in to. An agreement, sort of. I can never unhear that gasp. It wasn't the sound of my life flashing before me. It was the very human understanding that gravity was real and that I was about to fall and that nothing was going to catch me.

5.

I can never unhear Allen Iverson saying the word *practice*. On May 7, 2002, after being eliminated by the Celtics in the first round of the Eastern Conference Championship, Allen Iverson, who was the previous year's league MVP, gave a different kind of history-making performance: a press conference that lasted almost thirty minutes. For some NBA fans, like myself, Iverson represents a precise time in the sport when the league-small six-foot A.I. played with a conceit that realized miracles on the court, like his rookie year crossover against Michael Jordan. Iverson's signature crossover was the kind of basketball that could make anyone a fan of the game—the sort of speedy sparring that, even now when you watch clips of him play, unfolds as if there's a spotlight following him. There was no denying Allen Iverson, and so, when his 2002 press conference, following the 76ers' elimination from the playoffs and reports that he and coach Larry Brown were at odds with each other, aired, there was a sense that Iverson was working his on-court crossover, off court—choosing to spar with one reporter in particular who brought up the topic of Iverson's absence from one or two practice sessions. "I'm supposed to be the franchise player," he responded. "And we in here talking about practice? I mean listen, we're talking about *practice*. Not a game! Not a *game*! We're talking about *practice*. Not the game that I go out there and die for and play every game like it's my last, not the game, we're talking about practice, man. I mean, how silly is that? We're talking about *practice*."

Iverson says the sentence "We're talking about *practice*" no less than thirteen times, as if delegitimizing its implication with each slackened delivery of the word *practice*. Like Iverson freestyling with an opponent for a few seconds only to get low, fake right, and then make a quick crossover dribble to his left and lose a defender entirely, Iverson's press-conference dissidence was showy but earned. I can never hear the word *practice* uttered by anyone without Iverson's disenchanted tone hurtling to mind, because yes: What were they talking about? *Practice?*

6.

In the basement of the funeral home where family were soon to arrive, my mother, my aunt—my father's older sister—and my stepmother all gathered in a stark white room where my grandmother Thama was lying dead on a table wearing a white sweater blouse and petticoat.

That morning, my mother had asked if I wanted to join her later as she dressed my grandmother in the sari my aunt had brought—green with a gold trim is how I remember it, but I might be wrong. It could have been navy. I was seventeen at the time and said yes the way seventeen-year-olds say yes. I said, "Sure." Mostly, I was eager to witness my mother and stepmother in the same room. I was worried they might fight, that someone would yell. Nothing could have prepared me, though, for how silent those next twenty or so minutes would be.

I walked in behind them, shyly observed my dead grandmother, and proceeded to stand just beyond the door's threshold, attaching myself to the wall. There we were, five women, one dead.

My aunt unfolded the sari, and from that moment on, all I heard was: nothing. Nobody spoke. I will never unhear that nothing. It was the loudest nothing I've ever experienced.

Three women folding and tucking and pleating the silk sari. Forest green, now I remember. It was a subterranean green, darkening where the sari gathered and glimmering where the gold embroidery caught the room's awful fluorescent light. They lifted my grandmother and worked around her limp body with a delicate simpatico that was born right there and then. None of these women were particularly fond of one another, but they loved my Thama deeply. Circling her body, they were done quickly. I remember my aunt placing her hand on her mother's hand, and briefly, death was, I wanted to cry out, the most incredulous, excessive invention.

I rarely think of that room or the five of us in it—or should I say four? That silence, though, occasionally dawns on me. Noiselessness, I've come to learn, is simply how some memories age.

13

Upspeak

A T a wedding in Palm Springs, I met someone whom I'd only previously known through our correspondence online. He'd introduced himself to me four years prior, in an email that opened with, I think, our mutual love of certain film directors and, as it happens, our mutual roster of friends. Since we lived in separate cities, we'd Gchat and email, mostly about movies, and sometimes basketball, and our own projects too. At one point in 2012, we were each writing our own feature-length screenplays. We'd even made it to the second round of a writing-lab competition, and while we were excited for the other person, we weren't exactly demonstrative with our encouragement. It's possible I acted cagey when describing what my script was about—possessive to the point of sounding paranoid. Neither of us moved on to the third round. We stayed in touch.

Now it was May, some years into our correspondence.

We were both invited to the wedding of a mutual friend, who was marrying his longtime girlfriend. The plan was to meet in my hotel's lobby and, with another friend—not the one getting married—cab to a welcome dinner that functioned too as the rehearsal dinner.

In the lobby we hugged hello and continued casually, uneventfully, catching up. Speaking online for that many years had, I guess, doused all initial nerves. We talked about movies, basketball, how indiscriminately hot the desert is, and how happy we were for our friend who was getting married. I must have talked about palm trees—I can't help it when I'm in proximity to them. Palm trees pipe my sense of awe into its purest form. Puppies asleep on their sides, lattice piecrusts, and women in perfectly tailored pantsuits generate a similar response. So does young Al Pacino.

His "sad, lustrous, and doglike eyes," Lynne Tillman wrote in her 1992 *Sight and Sound* essay, "Kiss of Death," describing his performance as "Mikey" Corleone before he transforms into Michael Corleone, when he can still promise Diane Keaton, "That's my family, Kay. It's not me." Those young Pacino eyes capsize me. His battery of protean gestures is absorbing. Young Al Pacino makes me giddy. I sink into my chair. I experience the full-blown, bodily preoccupation of having a crush. Watching him is like discovering a long-lost audition tape, because his delivery, then, was intimate, kept, mild. I cover my face. I even once, not long ago, ducked under my desk while watching a scene from *The Panic in Needle Park*, before Bobby and

Helen—played with disconsolate, plain beauty by Kitty Winn—spiral downward together and before Helen is using, when they're just getting to know each other, actually. Because in this scene, Bobby is eating lunch with Helen, and he's smiling between sips from his can of Coke, and, well, who am I to survive that smile? The curl of his bottom lip is uncommonly expressive. The stillness of his voltage seduces. He tells Helen, "Don't just go around leaving people for no reason." The first time I saw *The Panic* was the first time I'd heard that sentiment expressed gently. Young Pacino is perfect as a small-time dealer whose speech is fleecy and whose walk is bright. He bounces like he just landed a backflip, like he might be attempting another one, like he doesn't know how to backflip at all but gets you thinking he can. Playing stickball and claiming he was once the "Babe Ruth of West Eighty-first Street," or lifting a TV from a van and impishly trying to pawn it off for more money than it's worth; or the way cigarettes and lollipops dangle from his mouth the same—all of these gestures, blink-moves, and hijinks reduce me to a ridiculous woman. Watching him in *Scarecrow*, grinning while he towel dries his hair, listening to Gene Hackman tell a story, I float into a state of feeling like my insides are sinking but my body is pirouetting ever so lightly, like a stray feather in no rush to touch down. The last time we ever see him so young is in the second *Godfather* when Fredo is ordering a banana daiquiri in Havana. Pacino, in those seconds, lets slip a smile only John Cazale could have drawn from him. I could go on. It wouldn't be hard. Young Al Pacino unsteadies me. Like young Al Pacino might say, *terrifically*.

But anyway. Palm trees. Palm Springs. The wedding. My online friend. For whatever reason, at the dinner and then the next day at the ceremony, and then following that, at the reception, I didn't spend much time with this friend I'd only known, up until now, through our emails. I was distracted. I was reunited with friends from college and dancing in gold sandals I rarely wear, and watching generations of one family dance together. How knees bending at funny angles and sweat mapping the same regions of a shirt are just as heritable as curly hair or a dry sense of humor.

At sunset, the San Jacinto Mountains turned pink-green shades of lithic tourmaline. It caught me off guard. Their likeness to rear-projection was an embarrassing reminder that I've limited my sense of panorama to city skylines. A city's horizon appears more spatial, believable, and substantive than do mountain ranges. I am mountain illiterate even though mountains are—like nature's narrative-build in general—the most legible telling of the story of time.

As the evening progressed, and as the venue's sequined strings of twinkle lights began blurring with purple bougainvillea vines, and as I was circuiting between the bar and other guests' untouched plates of cake, I knew it was soon time for bed. First, the hotel pool and then bed. It was a beautiful night.

A couple weeks after the wedding, the friend who'd shared the cab with us from the hotel to the rehearsal dinner texted me that my online friend had too started emailing with her. He told her it was nice to have finally met me but added, though I can't understand why, this next bit: he confessed to her that he was surprised by how high-pitched my voice was in person. When she told me what he'd said, I thought, *huh*. It seemed like the sort of pointless thing one says when trying to make a point without properly making it.

It's true. My voice is—I've been told on numerous occasions—unlikely. Childlike, almost. Not seductive. Informal. My voice is the voice of one's own voice when recorded. How it makes us cringe when we hear it. The pitch: elevated. Prohibitively hesitant at times—hooking declarative sentences into questions. I sound hasty. Unthinking. Like I have a wide frame of reference, of which I've fallen under the influence, but also of which I haven't considered with more depth, patience, time. I sound like the next-door neighbor in a situation comedy who always drops by uninvited. I sound like I'm wearing a backpack.

The older I get, the more my voice seems to disagree with what people perceive of me. Maybe they imagine a more serious tone. Modulated to reflect control. Or starched and matter-of-fact, like I'm reading aloud the instructions for assembling a bookshelf or slow-cooking beef stew. Or maybe people imagine that my voice would be silvery and pleasant. Maybe because in my own writing, descriptions of fruit, of women, of the changing light indoors play determining parts. As does vague melancholia, and the blow of failing to communicate. Perhaps every writer's long con is how openly she might write about joy, yet flops when experiencing it openly in her life.

While my voice doesn't bother me, how its inflection surprises people does. There are worse assumptions to be made, certainly. And yet, this one grates.

Still, I've wondered: Should I try to change my pitch? Should I try to sound more staid? I recently asked my father this question as we both stood in the kitchen, loitering in the quiet that follows a meal. He'd overheard me earlier in the day on a work call with one of my editors, during which I too had heard myself. There was, unfortunately, an echo I couldn't eliminate no matter how many times I tried dialing her again. I heard myself speak the entire call.

As my father and I stood in the kitchen, I asked him, unseriously, "How can I change my voice?"

Wiping the counter with a sponge, he thought for a moment. Then he looked up at me, smiling. "You know how to do it?"

"How?"

"Stop reacting to everything."

We laughed. But just as quick, I considered how depressing that would be. How regulating and unlike me to not be disposed to palm trees, the sharp pleats in a pantsuit, young Al Pacino. How unnecessarily held captive life would feel if I didn't react. If I wasn't susceptive and quick to greet what awakens me. My voice is, contrary to whatever insight accommodates how others think I *should* sound, the most *like* me. My least restrained quality, it rises and rejoices when the mood suits, and tendrils even when I'm doubtless. It's how I deliver. How I divulge. It's my noise. How it rises and falls, and then vaults. My "Oh yeah?" expresses confidence, like I'm willing to bet on something, but also "Oh yeah?"—as in, sincere interest, as in *Go on*. I could be voicing disbelief or absolute thrill when I begin a thought with "Apparently." Why give that up? The spoken dexterity.

From what's been expressed to me, my voice's junior quality, let's call it, could use a bad cold. A ballast. Some sobering. Some humility. A series of milestones that supposedly authorize a woman's voice.

On those days when I speak to no one until evening, when I've made plans with a friend, only for dinner, so as not to disturb the writing I hope will have been achieved— that so rarely ever is—it's on those days I forget I can speak. That I am capable of noise. I've spent hours molding the silent commotion in my head—a noise in and of itself, not sleek like a setting-loose but inharmonious, like rummaging—that to say anything more simply exhausts. Writing, like the hours that follow a concert, coats me with a static buzzing, well after I've closed my computer and rejoined the world. A day spent transmitting tendencies and chasing the occasional, phantom idea that hovers in front of me, only to disappear when I attempt to toss words on it, would—how could it not—take time to cast off. But when I sit down for dinner with a friend, and my first words do come out—cracked, slowed, and flat—and I think, *Isn't that nice?* my next reaction is to hurry and recover. To not savor, too warmly, this expected-of-me alternative. Those fixes I arrange myself into. How slippery it becomes to make amendments. The dicey irreparableness of being. I ask the waitress for some water. I clear my throat.

14

At My Least and Most Aware

NOT much has changed. I'm still a difficult woman who startles easy. I still forget to wash the apple before I eat it. I'm still oddly thankful for the rush of hot air let off from the sides of buses. Like things could be hotter, grosser. I'm still doubtful my stories possess a clear point. The sound of men gulping water still bothers me. I still interrupt. I'm still unprepared for how unusual it feels to receive a postcard; the traveled touch of card stock; of tapered handwriting chasing vertically up the side, allowing for a squished, tender sign-off. *Thinking of you. Miss you.* An unforeseen *Yours*. Even the faint sound of a postcard falling through my mail slot and landing on my floor is, somehow, still enchanted.

I still prefer counting to fourteen instead of ten. I still don't mind, perhaps I even like, ice cream's cold swallow rising up my throat so I can swallow it back down again. I still only have nightmares when I take naps. I still wonder what stops me, what version of me would exist had I let someone take my picture when I was younger, wearing a bikini with my hair up, while in the background an out-of-focus lake contrives to mislay the mood. Because hanging over pictures of lakes and girls and summer is the impression, often, of a missing person.

I still have trouble discerning between loneliness and solitude, and Sundays, and Schubert's sonatas. I'm still dismally unfunny; restless when I sit on grass; too much of a daughter to forget about the dead. Even though I own none, I still love the size of LP records. Their square, tactile bigness. And I still believe that people who buy them and collect them aren't snobs at all, but true blues. A record sleeve is unwieldy. To hold one is to sometimes appear like you're hugging one.

It still comes as a shock to me how irreversible life is. How there's no going back to whatever version of me existed before I saw *that* movie—the kind that switches me on to new streaks of consciousness by showing me a woman I feel strangely, formerly, acquainted with. Or watching Spielberg instill in me not a fear of sharks but a love for movie sound tracks and their wily, persuasive ploy to make my innermost thoughts sing. Or before I took pleasure in doing nothing, before I figured out there's no one way to live, before I tasted city smog outside another city's airport and knew right then that I was a city kid. Or before I felt my father weep into my arm the night his mother died, or took Angela's class fall semester and read Marguerite

Duras's account of a river and its current, a girl, a lover, a mother, of memory's weakness for women and gold lamé heels. Or when I was woken up by the news and this planet's despairing chorus—how it dislocates the heart and coaxes cynics and makes a mass out of individuals. Or whatever version of me existed before I met that boy whom I loved for one winter and well into spring, when the magnolias in early bloom looked not just pink but elaborate, ambient, and grand, like my insides were seeable— flowering so forcefully, like nature cautioning me: *Durga, this won't last.*

I still get shivers on the hottest summer days. I still think feeling startled, for instance, by a Post-it unsticking from my wall or by fluff flying in front of my nose is a subliminal reminder that I am alive and that being alive is a beta test full of little frights. I still confuse being misunderstood with feeling shame. I'm still hungriest when it's not quite dinner or when it's way past several bedtimes that would have allowed for a sensible sleep. I still believe it's impossible to experience anxiety sitting on a veranda and, contrary to popular imagery, possible to experience sharp panic in proximity to the ocean, the spray of waves, and the crescent sweep of a beach.

I still imagine my brain is peanut-sized, especially when I can't understand how bridges are built over large bodies of water; especially when I consider painters who paint hands that reflect a life and writers who thoughtfully clarify what is halfway known to them yet somehow lingering.

I'm still drawn to—since childhood—violet and lavender accents: hand towels in a guest bathroom; O'Keeffe's leaves and Elizabeth Taylor's eyes; the insides of Dumbo's ears; Sherbrooke metro's louvered ceilings; Helen Frankenthaler's rinsed, puddled shores. Agnès Varda in a crowd.

Recently, my mother said to me while driving, "People don't change." I had just seen someone from my past, and the encounter had been tense and artificial. We labored, he and I, over niceties. Listening to him felt like work. It was as though we were both trying to retrieve a mutual tenderness that had fallen from our hands and rolled into a storm drain. How unfamiliar it now was to merely look at him, and as it happens, unresolved arguments that now felt colorless managed to creep back in. We weren't fighting so much as reusing old motivations to rile the other person up. Like testing to see if they still worked. It was, I'll concede, wonderfully juvenile. Unfortunately, the verbal construction of rehashing—of jaggedly saying something again and again, just differently—debilitates. We returned to that whole district of emotions, long forgotten. It was unavailing. Impaired and confining. It's bunker-speak. "Let me rephrase" might be the tautest way to try to win someone over.

So I listened to this person I once called "Baby, Boy, Babe" until I'd hit my limit or, perhaps, found my stride. I interrupted and said something rude. Cutting, cruel, and unnecessary. How else to protect the momentum I'd accumulated over the last little while? I'm sure there's a better way to do it—to be gracefully immune—and yet, these rare mutinous flashes are satisfying. We both agreed it had been unwise to meet up. "A bad idea," he said. *Foolish*, I later told my mother.

"I'm telling you," my mother insisted while we were stopped at a red light. "People don't change." My mother was, I gathered, speaking about someone from her past in order to empathize with mine. It's been lovely in adulthood to share this changed design for connecting with my parents. I am now in possession of a history that, like theirs, often pulls. We can relate without laying bare all the details. Like speaking *alongside*; a new responsiveness that doesn't pry.

Because even though I am still their youngest—taller, wiser, yet happiest when I am barefoot in their home eating sliced fruit—I have outlived an impasse; many even. I can identify what constitutes a dilemma, a big drama, and the difference between the latter and a minor, reparable scrape. Like the stuff that goes on in those early-morning hours, eased by tequila's burn and a decoy debt to stay out. Like the hurt we cause when we've been enduring too much in silence and have started to trust our own fixed claim that everything is okay.

But being barefoot in my parents' home. Eating fruit. Standing barefoot just outside the front door. Is there a symbol for *return* more comprehensive than that? It's pleasure

mingled with nostalgia and the quick fix shelter provides—
how it lightens but also strikes at the heart. How standing
barefoot on the steps outside is repossessing for both the
parent who is admiring and the child—now grown—who
has come around to "home," not just as a place but as an
idea she can tend to. A belief that it's possible to let one's
guard down and enjoy the emotional knowledge that orbits
a home and the memories, while not all good, that confirm
her. The sound of onions browning on the stove and the
charismatic flop of a daughter's shoes kicked off by the door
safeguard the story of a family.

But.

But. While my mother said, "People don't change,"
what she meant is, I'd estimate: I shouldn't try to change a
person. That the effort exerted is often ineffectual and upsetting. Nobody adjusts himself or herself, unless prompted
first, by some interior gurgling. Some deep mobilizing.
Urgency forms in the belly. And change, I've come to understand, rises up like nausea: the promise of relief is what
makes it bearable. The body's clever ways for communicating shifts can make a person crazy, but also move a person
toward life.

In suggesting I shouldn't attempt to alter how this
person from my past thinks or finds his focus, my mother
also meant: Be wary of overvaluing what he gives. Be cautious of how proportioned my ability to love is with how
impressionable I become. What moves him to create belongs
discretely to him. What lights him up from inside and in-

cites growth is what will ultimately specify his dimension. Not me.

I think that's what my mother meant, anyway. And as she kept driving and our talk turned to dinner, I stayed half present, obligated to my nerve center and that funny way a car's window offers a scrim for me to solemnize and star in some mini scenario. To emotionally migrate yet stay put. Because the gray zip of highway, those accompanying blimp clouds, and a passing swath of people all provide the perfect blur for seeing things not as they stand but as I'd like them to, in time, reel out.

What is it about moving on that maroons me? What is it about recuperating from a failed relationship that feels nearest to a slow-drip, unconcealed crack-up? Are the many lives we've lived immortal? And which is more crucial: That I regenerate or that I carry? That I hold true, build upper-body strength, expand on my catalog of what I consider fun, or wear more navy because it's not quite black and faintly adjusts frame of reference, and hesitates between looking meant and like a mistake. Or do I squarely retain this person—his textures, how he concentrated my world. Or do I develop an improved tendency for reclaiming myself? Do I double over, obsess, fly in the face of, listen to my mother, be still?

I'm not sure what I believe. That not much has changed is, all at once, off-putting and also pleasing. Like reinforcements. Even the bad bits, like the boy I used to call Boy. Whom I still care about and think about, particularly when there's nobody else I'd rather sit next to on those strange afternoons when freak dread sends nameless pangs my way and all I want is a person to be my pillow so I might feel less random, spinning, negligible. A person who listens while I don't finish my thoughts because maintaining completeness grows tiresome. A person so acquainted with my treasury of reluctance, with the lines of my body, that I forget I have one, and he forgets he has one, and limbs become logs to rest our heads on, and are we even people anymore? Or merely two souls whose condition is best described as "awaiting clearance."

Or, perhaps, the only way to track change is to acknowledge these constants as a criterion that habituates me. I'll always need those steps outside my parents' home—some aspect or imprecise concept of them—where I can sit and watch the light dim as the evening breeze makes nice with the day's complaints, and as I hear a small dog jingling before I see him trot past, and as my appetite builds because just inside, so amazingly close, are my parents cooking dinner. The sound of which has never changed. Utensils sliding in a drawer, the fridge opening and sealing closed, a knife's *thwack*, the slight chime of glasses knocking against plates, the quick shuffle to make room at the table for something piping hot, and the loving "Careful!" that strikes curt.

The many overall movements of a home, required to sit down and eat, are, especially with family, somehow impersonal. Particular yet detached. Everything becomes concrete. The fork is a familiar fork. The clatter is mindless. Potatoes are matter-of-fact. There is love; it lives in the practical details. A family is more than it shows. That the future's unspecified terms provide a few recognizable basics, and that I might find, somewhere in me, a tension—the good kind—for tapping into what springs me forward, is, I reason, the hope. The discord, the din, what stays the same, what reappears, what's underneath, the misremembered and all there is to fathom. Growing up, for a long period that's not worth mentioning here, I thought the expression was "Play it by *year*." As in, take your time. A whole year. More. Whatever you need. There's no rush.

Acknowledgments

Thank you to my editor, Emily Bell, for her willingness and heart. For understanding this project's roving, inconclusive zigzags even when I didn't. Thank you to Maya Binyam for her thoughtful notes, often near-telepathic. Thank you to Jonathan Galassi, who wasted no time and asked me what *I* wanted to make real. Thank you to Rodrigo Corral. Thank you, FSG.

Luc Sante, thank you for getting this whole thing going. Dayna Tortorici, for suggesting this title was not someone else's but in fact mine.

I am grateful to Gaylord Neely, Chris and Carla, and November in Provincetown. Thankfulness to Lena Dunham for counsel and reading early drafts. Kim Witherspoon for her strong, good sense and for inspiring in me new exciting wants. Hilton Als, for Christmas and for reminding me to keep those near who allow me to hear the voice in my head. Tavi Gevinson for the walks, the correspondence, the nook, the deep love and care you give to connecting.

Some minor changes were made to previously published essays, those edited by Doree Shafrir, Mark Lotto, Jessica Grose, and Haley Mlotek. Thank you for saying, *Run with it*.

Acknowledgments

Sarah Nicole Prickett: I'm so happy that we met. Isn't it wonderful when we're in different time zones? When we get four chances at 11:11? Thank you for being maddeningly good at finding, in your words, *the stray gesture.* Teddy Blanks, thank you for encouraging me to write about what's off to the side. For going to the movies with me.

Collier Meyerson, Jenny Zhang, Doreen St. Felix, my sisters in daughterhood: You've been so impactful. Thank you for how you write and what you write about. For introducing me to your families. What a privilege. Katherine Bernard for re-centering me when this project needed it. Fiona Duncan for sending me into outer space.

Thank you Max Neely Cohen for book talk, ball talk, reassuring me through this process, and answering all my questions no matter what time of day.

Gratitude to Echo Hopkins, Tait Foster, India Nicholas, Rachel Levy, Bryn Little, Mark and Deirdre Silverman, Jackie Linton, Lucy Morris, Heben Nigatu, Ayesha Siddiqi, Amy Rose Spiegel, Ross Scarano, Ashley Ford, Jazmine Hughes, Sam Axelrod, Ian Blair, Dana Drori, Marcelo Gomes (Dear M., the conversations, so many that we've had, are in here), Katie Baker, Judnick Mayard, Arabelle Sicardi, Cord Jefferson, Akiva Gottlieb, Zoë Worth, Almitra Corey, Jesse Klein, Lauren Smythe, Vinson Cunningham, Monika Woods, and Brian Morton.

My family—from day one and as we grow—Dolores, Rana, Lisa, Mritiunjoy, Siraj, Kim, and Willis. I'd be spinning or stuck doing something I don't love if it weren't for you. You are my light.